OLD AUSTRAL

The People, the Pastimes, the Pioneering Spirit

The Five Mile Press

The Five Mile Press Pty Ltd
1 Centre Road, Scoresby, Victoria 3179 Australia
www.fivemile.com.au

First published 2009
This paperback edition first published 2012

Reprinted 2012, 2013

Printed in China

Designed by Zoë Murphy

Front cover: Sydney GPO and Martin Place, c. 1911
Spine: Outback Family, c. 1880s
Back cover: Settler's Wife and Children, c. 1890
Previous page: Welcoming the Anzacs Home, 1919

The photographs in this book are part of a larger collection of out-of-copyright images taken by largely unknown photographers and used by The Five Mile Press in a collection of books entitled *The Centenary Collection* (2000). Every effort has been made to identify the photographers used in this book. If anyone has further information, please contact the publisher.

National Library of Australia Cataloguing-in-Publication entry
Sheppard, Barrie
Old Australia : the people, the pastimes and the pioneering
spirit / Barrie Sheppard.

9781743461532 (pbk.)
Australians--Pictorial works.
Australia--Social life and customs--Pictorial works.
Australia--Description and travel--Pictorial works.
994.032

Aboriginal and Torres Strait Island community members are advised that this book contains images of deceased persons.

CONTENTS

Opposite page: *Prime Minister Stanley Bruce and his wife, Ethel, Canberra, 1928*
Overleaf: *A typist, a bookkeeper and high-stool clerks, busy in the corporate office of the early 1900s*

— INTRODUCTION —

$\mathcal{M}$uch has changed since the British established the colony of New South Wales on the shores of Sydney Harbour in January 1788. From that first colony, and the later settlements at Hobart, Melbourne, Brisbane, Adelaide and Perth, settlers moved inland to occupy the land, displacing the original Indigenous inhabitants.

In time, those founding white settlements grew into large vibrant cities, and many small country settlement towns became prosperous, some developing into large regional cities. The wealth of the pastoral and agricultural industries, the fabulous riches of the goldfields, and the growth of manufacturing made this growth possible. And then, politically, in 1901 the six colonies, which had been granted self-government by Britain in the nineteenth century, federated to form the Commonwealth of Australia we know today.

During this period, particularly the latter part of the nineteenth and the early twentieth centuries, great social, cultural and technological changes occurred. One significant technological advance, one that made possible books of this kind, was the invention and development of the camera. Before its advent, the visual recording of history had had to rely on the pencil, ink and paint of the artist.

Old Australia, drawing on the skill of those early photographers, brings together a collection of scenes of early Sydney and Melbourne, of the goldfields, and of aspects of life generally, including working, recreational and family life.

Barrie Sheppard

SYDNEY TOWN

From its Georgian origins, Sydney, the golden sandstone city, developed through the vibrant industrial age of the Victorian era to become the great world harbour city of the south.

George Street took its name from George III, the reigning King of England at the time of British settlement. This impressive, nearer row of commercial premises is in the later Colonial Regency style, the more decorative period of the Prince Regent, later George IV. Note the elaborate pediments on the Peapes building. Sydney was the first Australian city to electrify its cable tram system – electrification beginning in 1898. Other road traffic is exclusively horse-drawn – the motor vehicle is still a decade away. Two streetsweepers have stepped back to make way for the tram and the two gentlemen in the buggy. Horse buses can be seen behind the second tram.

George Street, Sydney, New South Wales, c. 1900

2

KERRY. PHOTO. SYDNEY.

3201. GEORGE ST. NEAR HUNTER STREET.

*T*his wider section of George Street is host to Sydney's proud civic centre. Commanding the space is the Sydney Town Hall, replete with imposing clock tower and lantern. Completed in 1889, the building was designed by John Wilson, Albert Bond and others in the sumptuous Second Empire style. The mansard-roofed pavilion, just visible, is a telltale sign; so too are the intricate decoration of its surfaces and the profuse, ornamental detailing of the parapets. To its right is St Andrew's Anglican Cathedral. Gothic in style, it was built to address a planned square to the west, which, unfortunately, never materialised. To the north is the Queen Victoria Markets Building (now the Queen Victoria Building), completed in 1898. Its huge domes signal its Federation Romanesque styling.

George Street at the Sydney Town Hall, c. 1900

In early colonial Sydney, Queen's Square was at the centre of state and church power, symbolised by the statue of Queen Victoria that was added in 1888. Behind the imperious queen is St James' Anglican Church, the second church built in New South Wales and now the oldest standing. Built by convict architect Francis Greenway for Governor Macquarie, its elegant geometry and beautifully proportioned forms make it a masterpiece of Colonial Regency design. The building was originally designed as a courthouse, but was converted during early construction. Nearby (out of frame), stands the Hyde Park Barracks, now a museum, and the former Sydney Infirmary and Dispensary (the 'Rum Hospital'), part of which was converted to a parliamentary chamber in 1829.

St James' Church, King Street, Sydney, c. 1890

Housing conditions for Sydney's poor in 1900 were appalling. Ripe for the spread of disease, slum housing harboured the bubonic plague that broke out in Sydney in January 1900. The disease, introduced by rats leaving ships in the harbour, claimed 303 victims within eight months. One hundred and three died. Large areas of Sydney were quarantined and disinfected, and hundreds of suspected carriers forcibly incarcerated on North Head. Houses and out-buildings in slum areas were demolished. Those in the Rocks area didn't always escape demolition, but if they did, they were cleared later to make way for the southern approach to the Sydney Harbour Bridge. In 1901, eight hundred houses were acquired by the Sydney Harbour Trust.

Cumberland Street, The Rocks, Sydney, c. 1900

Until 1906, Redfern Station was Sydney's principal hub for land passenger transport. Trams and horse-drawn vehicles converged there to convey passengers from the railway terminus to and from the city centre. Built originally in 1851, its one platform was eventually increased to fourteen. However, by the end of the century the station was considered too far from the heart of the city. In 1906, when the new, grand Central Station was completed, Redfern Station was demolished. The station at Everleigh, 1.3 kilometres downline, was enlarged and renamed 'Redfern'. The Redfern area was named after William Redfern, a convict transported to New South Wales for mutiny. He later worked as a surgeon in the colony, and in 1816 took charge of the former Sydney Infirmary and Dispensary (the 'Rum Hospital'), so-called because it was financed using the profits of the rum trade.

Redfern Station, Sydney, 1902

It's not difficult to see why the Pyrmont Bridge across Darling Harbour's Cockle Bay was a main thoroughfare between Sydney and the west until it was superseded by the modern freeway system. Opened in 1902, the bridge has two central swing spans that enable shipping to pass. They were the largest swing spans in the world and the first to be electrically operated. At a London conference of the Institute of Civil Engineers in 1907, the bridge was acclaimed a 'marvel of modern engineering'. In 1980, it was closed permanently to vehicular traffic and shipping, but reopened as a pedestrian way when the Darling Harbour entertainment and tourist complex was completed in 1988.

The Pyrmont Bridge, Sydney, 1902

K.& CO.

329. PYRMONT BRIDGE

The high-rise buildings shown here place this scene firmly in the 1920s. The development of steel-framed building construction in the late nineteenth century freed the wall of a building from its load-bearing function, and gave birth to the modern skyscraper. With the advent of the Otis elevator, only the technology of fire-safety services of the time placed limits on building heights. The Art Deco styling – the strong cornices contrasting with the soaring verticals, and the geometric elements detailing the buildings' surfaces – is also typical of the 1920s. The men's clothing and the motor vehicles confirm the period, and there's not a horse-drawn vehicle to be seen.

The Bridge and Loftus Street Corner, Sydney, 1920s

The western face of this section of George Street mirrors the splendours of European Renaissance architecture. The window treatments of the Robertson & Co bookshop building draw heavily on neoclassical motifs from both Ancient Greece and Rome. Its neighbour, on the other hand, is modelled on the fourteenth century Florentine palazzo. Note the rusticated ground level floor and the elaborated treatment of its second floor – its piano nobile or 'noble floor'. Then, on the building beyond, the mansard roof, decorative columns and opulent detailing reflect the glory of France's Second Empire embellishment of Renaissance style. And passing it all, in humble contrast, trundles all manner of Sydney's horse-drawn traffic – jinkers, horse trams, delivery lorries and hansom cabs.

George Street, Looking South from the GPO, Sydney, c. 1900

Circular Quay is built on the site where Governor Phillip landed in January 1788 to establish the colony of New South Wales. The Quay was originally named Semi-Circular Quay, but the name was shortened for convenience. All passenger ferry services on Sydney Harbour and the Parramatta River terminate at the Quay. The Manly Beach terminal is clearly visible. Passenger ships and cargo vessels also berthed at docks on its western side. The Quay was also the terminal for all Sydney tram services to the eastern suburbs. The trams shown here would have parked overnight in tram sheds on nearby Bennelong Point. The tram depot was demolished in 1958 to make way for the Sydney Opera House.

Trams at Circular Quay, Sydney, 1930s

The crowd milling around the GPO reflects the more relaxed life of the Edwardian era – more relaxed, that is, than the Victorian age it replaced. The cut of the men's suits is surprisingly modern, as are their fedoras and racy straw boaters. For the women, the constraining crinoline has given way to a looser, more free-flowing skirt. Colours, though, are still dark. Designed by the New South Wales government architect, James Barnet, the GPO was built in stages between 1866 and 1891. With its encircling colonnade and imposing clock tower, this classical masterpiece inspired the redevelopment of the precinct in a style and confidence more in keeping with Barnet's creation. In 1996, the interior of the building was converted into boutique shops, restaurants and other nightlife entertainments.

Sydney GPO and Martin Place, 1911

Sydney is blessed with magnificent surf beaches in its metropolitan area. Here at Coogie on a summer's day, Sydneysiders enjoy the beach – up to a point. Even though the law prohibiting bathing in daylight (even in a neck-to-knee bathing costume) had been relaxed by this time, many of those who have ventured in remain fully clothed. Most just stand about in their Edwardian suits, dresses and hats, taking what relief they can from the sea breeze. The scene is clearly pre-1924: there is no sign of the huge Coogie Beach Amusement Pier, constructed that year. The pier, which had extended 180 metres into the sea, was demolished in 1934 because it could not withstand the force of the Coogie surf.

Coogie Beach, Sydney, 1909

This is how the site of the present New South Wales Parliament building looked in 1870. Then it was the Sydney Infirmary and Dispensary, built by Governor Macquarie in 1813 on the proceeds of the rum trade. It became known as the Rum Hospital. In an attempt to control the notorious rum trade, Macquarie gave surgeon D'Arcy Wentworth, pastoralist Alexander Riley and merchant Garnham Blazwell an exclusive licence to import rum, provided they used the profits to build the hospital. Macquarie's attempt to wipe out the illegal trade in rum failed, but the colony did gain a hospital. Part of the building was used to house the colony's Mint, and in 1829 the New South Wales Legislative Council chamber was housed in the surgeons' quarters of the hospital.

Sydney Infirmary and Dispensary, 1870

SYDNEY INFIRMARY DEC. 1870

*P*otts Point, on the harbour a few kilometres east of the Sydney Harbour Bridge, was named after Joseph Potts, an accountant with the Bank of New South Wales, now Westpac. He purchased 2.6 hectares of land there from the Judge Advocate, Joseph Wylde. The point quickly became dotted with the mansions of the rich, including Elizabeth Bay House, Sydney's finest Colonial Georgian residence. The man in the photograph, enjoying the view across the harbour, strikes a pose reminiscent of a figure looking across the Seine in a famous French painting of the time – *Bathers at Asnières* by neo-impressionist artist Georges Seurat. The photographer may have had the Seurat picture in mind when he composed his picture.

Potts Point, Sydney, c. 1890

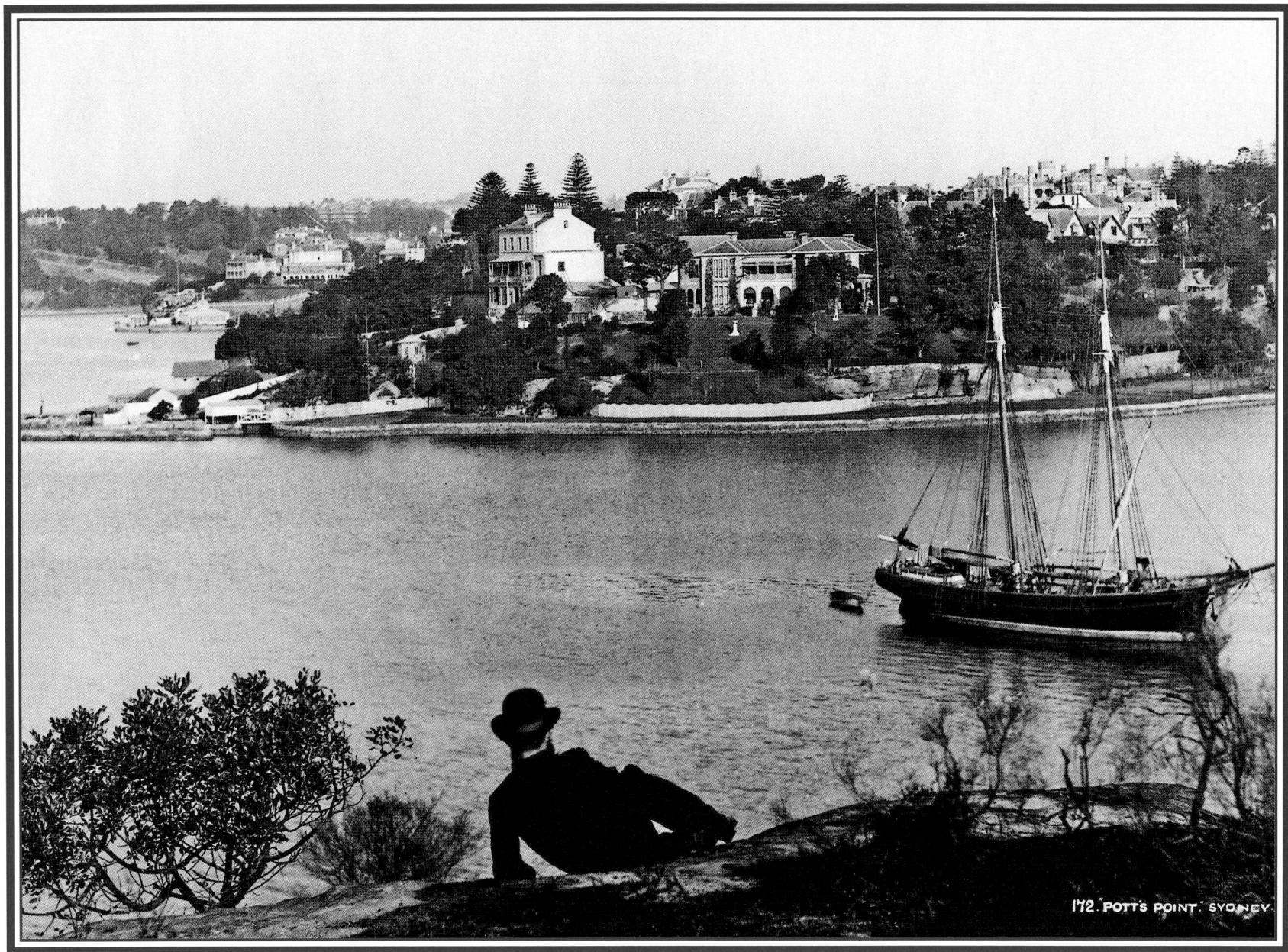

172. POTT'S POINT. SYDNEY.

Sydney's underground railway was designed by James Bradfield, designer of the Sydney Harbour Bridge and one of Australia's finest civil engineers of the time. The first section, from Central Station to St James via a station at Museum, was begun in 1924 and completed in 1926. An extension to Circular Quay was completed in 1931. In 1934, coinciding with the opening of the Sydney Harbour Bridge, a second line connected North Shore lines with Central, via stations at Wynyard and Town Hall. Shown here is the excavation for Museum Station, constructed using the 'cut and cover' method. There are no giant tunnelling augers, mechanical diggers and front-end scoops used here – just human muscle, aided by dynamite, picks, shovels and horse power.

Sydney Underground Construction, 1925

— GOLD FEVER —

*The discovery of gold in New South Wales and Victoria in the 1850s,
and later in Queensland and Western Australia, sparked huge gold rushes.
Diggers poured in to the diggings from all over the world, and countless city
and farm workers downed tools to seek their fortunes on the goldfields.*

Extracting alluvial gold from stream beds at the diggings was technologically simple, but it required hard work and persistence. Panners swilled tin dishes of gravel to wash away the lighter material and leave the heavier gold dust in the pan, if they were lucky. The cradle, an American invention, was a little more sophisticated. Gravel was shovelled into a hopper, which was then rocked as water was poured in. The finer, heavier particles were sieved through the bottom onto a riffled tray designed to trap the coarser grit. Small nuggets could then be picked out, but the finer material had to be panned to separate any gold dust from the residue.

Cradling and Panning, Gembrook, Victoria, 1880s

When water is more valuable than gold, as it was at Coolgardie in the 1890s, dry methods are needed to separate alluvial gold from paydirt. In the contraption shown here, the paydirt was shovelled into the hopper, which was then shaken to feed the dirt through holes in its floor. Hand-operated bellows blew away the lighter dirt. The gold remained on the inclined, ribbed tray below. The technique, similar to the winnowing of grain, was called dry-blowing. It wasn't the best of methods, and made a tough life even more difficult for the diggers. But here, they are happy to examine their find for the camera.

Dry Blowing at Coolgardie, Western Australia, c. 1895

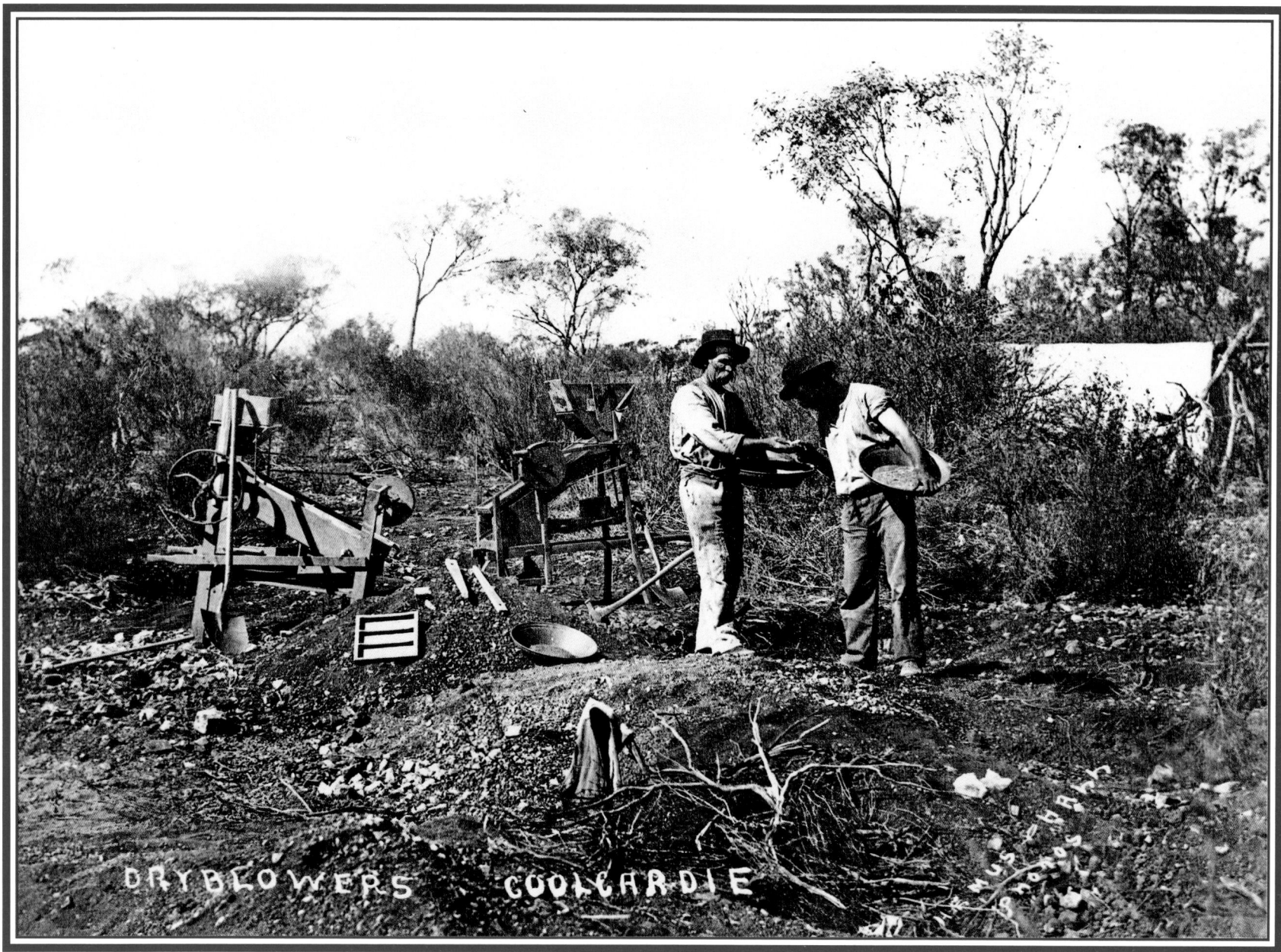

DRYBLOWERS COOLGARDIE

The Ballarat gold rush began in 1851. By 1854 the population of the town had soared to 47,000. Wealth poured out of the diggings to the Treasury in Melbourne. Elegant Sturt Street testifies to that wealth. The grand Neo-Renaissance town hall, with its Second Empire clock tower, stands as a symbol of the town's wealth and civic pride. So, too, do the fine street gas lamps and the other Victorian buildings lining the boulevard, replete with their add-on colonial verandas. The street cabbies have congregated at a time just prior to the installation of a public, horse-drawn tramway system in 1887. Fifty horses pulled a fleet of eighteen trams (seventeen double-deckers) along Ballarat's streets, much to the consternation of the cab operators, who obstructed them whenever possible.

Sturt Street, Ballarat, Victoria, 1880s

The departure of the gold escort from Coolgardie for the trek across 550 kilometres of lonely, arid country to Perth was an event worth witnessing. Here, lined up in front of the Union Bank as if to protect it, men of the town watch the departure. The frail buggy, though, looks more vulnerable, despite its escort of one trooper riding shotgun, another mounted. Western Australian gold escorts from Coolgardie, however, were not plagued by bushrangers as those in eastern Australia had been earlier in the century. The coming of the railway to Coolgardie in 1896 obviated the need for the kind of gold transport shown in the photograph.

Gold Escort, Coolgardie, Western Australia, c. 1890

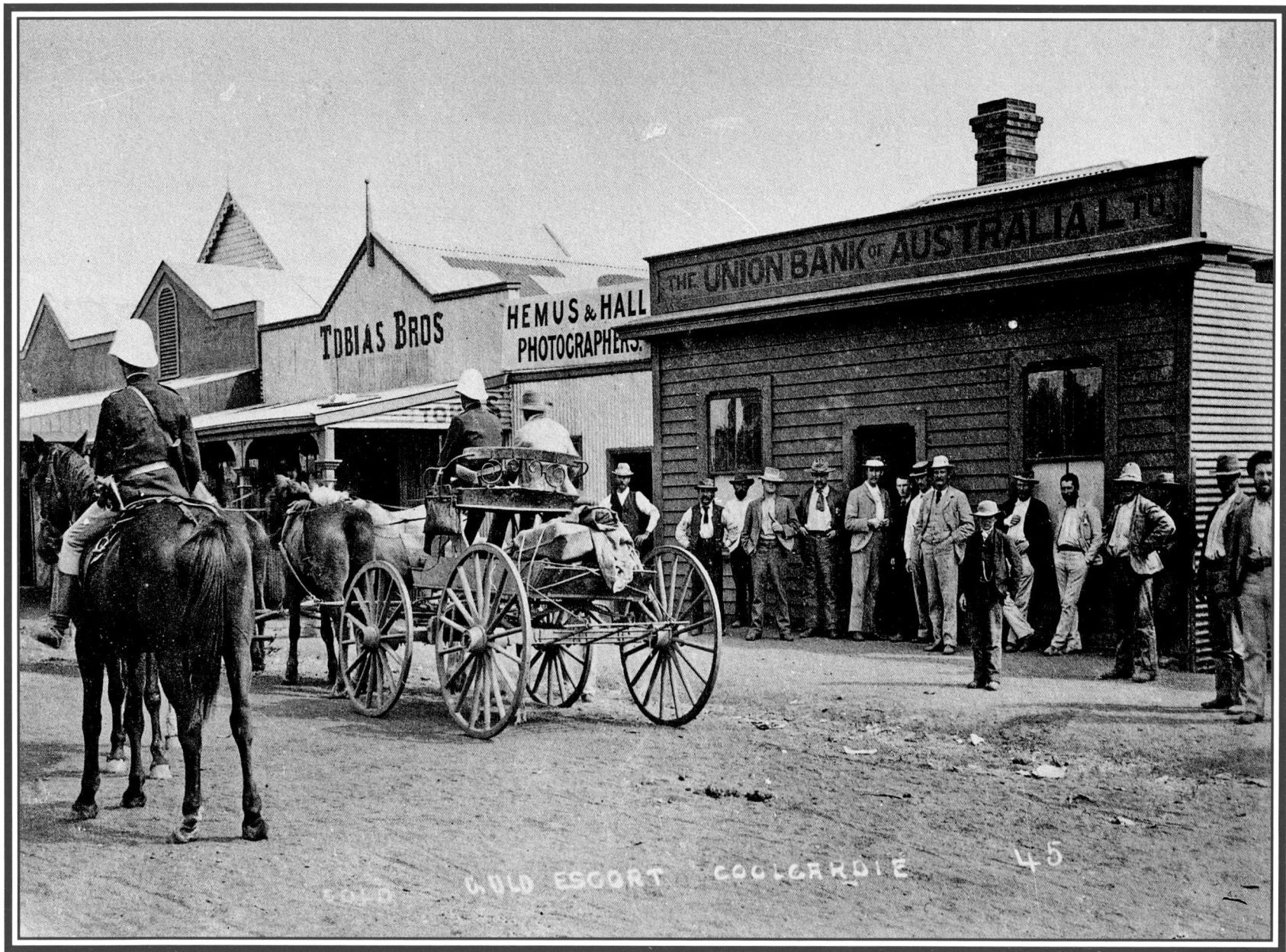

GOLD ESCORT COOLGARDIE 45

*I*n 1870, shepherd Tom Saunders discovered gold on the Guntawang cattle run. The find sparked a rush and the town of Gulgong was born. The family of the young Henry Lawson was part of the rush. The town was known as a 'poor man's diggings'. However, diggers, rich and poor alike, liked to drink. Gulgong had numerous hotels, some with billiard saloons, others with music halls and other entertainments. The town even had an opera house, which functions to this day. The Queensland Hotel, on the main street, was one of the more popular drinking holes. Proprietor Wright provided his patrons with a gas lamp to guide their way at night, but even in broad daylight he appears not to have lacked customers.

Queensland Hotel, Gulgong, New South Wales, 1872

*G*old was discovered in Coolgardie by Edward Bayley in 1892, sparking a gold rush from eastern Australia, then in the grip of a severe depression. By 1898, the population of Coolgardie had risen to 15,000, making it the largest town in Western Australia after Perth and Fremantle. Although the railway came to the town in 1896, coach travel still served the bustling centre. Here, outside the coach depot, Bayley Street is cluttered with coaches, cabs, and passengers arriving and departing. Above the Billiard Saloon, the Union Jack, flag of the British Empire, and the two flanking colonial flags date the photograph clearly in pre-Federation times.

Bayley Street, Coolgardie, Western Australia, 1896

*J*ames Leggatt knew that fortunes were to be made on the goldfields in ways other than by mining. Diggers must eat, and meat was a staple of their diet. In Gulgong he had two shops: this one open to the street, the other a more substantial edifice with a boarded front. But in both shops carcasses were displayed in the open. There being no refrigeration, meat had to be eaten quickly, or preserved by salting or smoking. Carcasses of sheep sold at tuppence a pound, and the best steaks for fourpence a pound. Leggatt extended his service out of town using his butchers' carts. He named his business after the Smithfield meat market in London, and a similarly named market near Sydney.

Leggatt's Butchery, Smithfield Branch, Gulgong, New South Wales, 1872

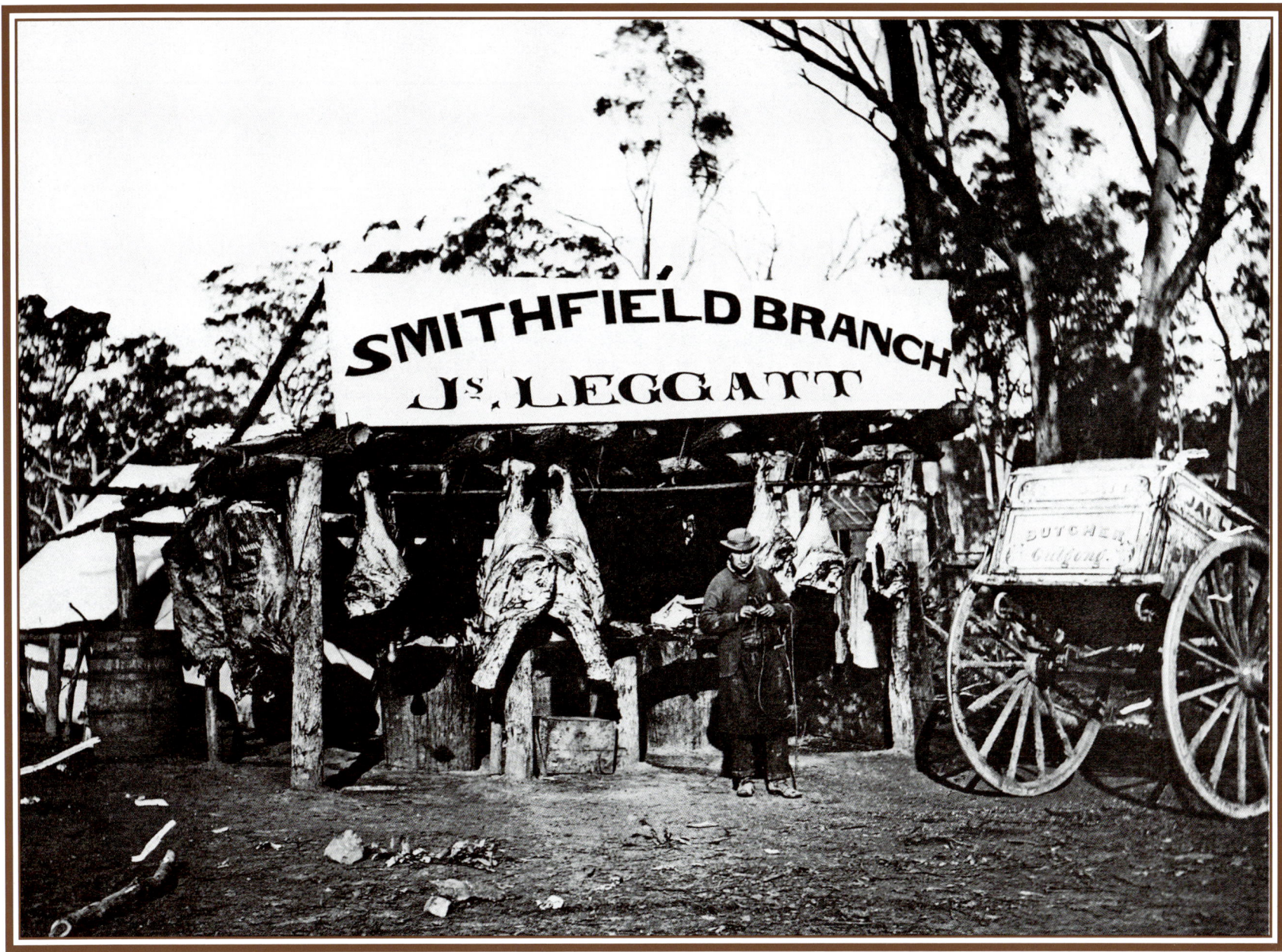

This giant Garfield Water Wheel of the Crushing Works at Forest Creek at Chewton near Castlemaine was built in 1887. Gold-bearing rock was mined from underground shafts and transported to the crushing works by horse-drawn drays. The water wheel, at a diameter of approximately twenty-five metres, dominated the landscape and made dwarfs of the mill workers seen here. The rim of the wheel consisted of 220 iron buckets. Water was channelled into the buckets, turning the wheel slowly in an anti-clockwise direction. Its revolving central shaft was connected to a system of levers that lifted and dropped fifteen stone stampers. Gold was then extracted from the crushed ore using cyanide.

Forest Creek Crushing Works, Chewton, Victoria, 1880s

Gold was discovered in Bendigo in 1851. Initially, most of the gold was alluvial. Mining soon denuded the wooded hills and scarred the terrain with mullock heaps, not to mention a scatter of tents, crude huts and mining equipment. But by the 1860s deep-lead methods were more prominent, a method requiring substantial capital. Five thousand shafts totalling ninety kilometres honeycombed the diggings. The substantial, two-storey residence in the background (left) of the photograph is that of wealthy mine owner Mr George Lansell. For the rest, the scene is a hotchpotch of miners' cottages, shops, public buildings, mine-head frames and steam-driven crushing works. There's little evidence of town planning!

Bendigo, Victoria, 1860s

With the discovery of rich gold-bearing reefs deep beneath the surface of alluvial goldfields, large mining companies took out leases on land for deep-lead mining. Diggers, though, retained their right to stake claims to mine nearer the surface on the company's leasehold. But their claims, usually about fifty square metres, had to be fifty feet (approximately sixteen metres) from the edge of the reef. The leaseholder was required to define the line of the reef. Disputes inevitably arose about its exact position. Here a large group of miners at Coolgardie have gathered to witness such a dispute. One digger seems quite sure about where the reef line runs.

Trouble Over a Claim, Coolgardie, Western Australia, 1899

Alluvial Trouble 1898
Diggers Meeting 170
Ivanhoe Venture Dwyer

Not all of those who flocked to the goldfields during the rushes went to seek their fortune in gold. Entrepreneurial men knew that money was to be made supplying the diggers and their families, not only with mining equipment, but also with food, drink and household goods. A careful examination of the interior of this general store, one of sixty in Coolgardie, shows a huge range of goods stocked by the owner. There's all manner of household hardware, tea from India and Ceylon, Swallow and Ariell biscuits, tinned and bottled food and drink, and even encyclopaedias, to name just a few. The trunks, dominating the shop floor, suggest that many Coolgardians left the fields carrying much more than they came with.

General Store, Coolgardie, Western Australia, 1890s

Thousands of alluvial gold diggers scrabbling and washing dirt in desert country will soon create a vista resembling a moonscape. In the late 1880s the flat and barren Teetulpa fields, halfway between Port Augusta and Broken Hill, attracted more diggers than any other South Australian field, before or since. Aboriginal men, some shown here, joined the rush. Life for the diggers was harsh. No firewood meant there was little protection against the freezing desert nights, and a lack of water meant diggers had to use inefficient and ineffective dry-blowing methods to separate gold dust from paydirt. Only when the government built a dam and a condensation plant did things improve, but not before a typhoid outbreak had killed three men.

Washing Dirt at Teetulpa, South Australia, 1886

Brady's gully

Water was liquid gold in Kalgoorlie and Coolgardie in the late 1890s. It had to be carted forty kilometres and retailed at one shilling per gallon. To supply the exploding population and the thirsty goldmines, the Western Australian government built the Goldfields Water Supply Scheme. It was the brainchild of public works engineer DY O'Connor. From the purpose-built Mundaring Weir near Perth, 23,000 cubic metres of water were pumped daily through eight pumping stations along 540 kilometres of pipe to the goldfields. Here, workmen lower one of the 8.5 metre lengths of interlocking pipe into place. Sadly, as a result of criticism from the press and politicians, O'Connor committed suicide in 1902, before the pipeline was completed.

Laying the Water Pipeline to Coolgardie, Western Australia, 1902

In 1860, the Victorian Exploration Expedition Committee brought six camels from northern India to Victoria. They were for use as transport for the Burke and Wills expedition across the continent from Melbourne to the Gulf of Carpentaria. Cameleers also came to tend the camels. A steady influx of cameleers from Afghanistan and what is now Pakistan followed. For over fifty years, camels played a crucial role in Australian inland transportation. It wasn't until the advent of the motor truck in the early twentieth century that the picturesque camel trains faded from the Australian desert scene. Here, before the construction of the goldfields pipeline, Afghanis and others load water for transport to the water-starved diggings of Coolgardie and Kalgoorlie.

Ships of the Desert Load Water for the Diggings, Western Australia, 1890s

MARVELLOUS MELBOURNE

*With a population of 500,000 in the 1880s, Melbourne was the largest city in the
British Empire, after London. Built on the wealth of the gold rushes of the
1850s and 60s, the city was a bustling, booming Victorian metropolis,
popularly known at the time as 'Marvellous Melbourne'.*

In the nineteenth century, Collins Street was an elegant boulevard defined by a variety of sumptuous Victorian buildings –
domestic, commercial, institutional and ecclesiastical. Here at its eastern end, a cable tram trundles past a waiting cabman. Already
the plane trees that give the street its leafy character today have been established. Prosperous medical professionals, as well as artists,
practised and lodged at this so-called 'Paris End'. Tom Roberts painted his iconic work *Shearing the Rams* in his studio at number 95.
Unfortunately, development in the 1960s and 70s destroyed much of Collins Street's Victorian splendour.

Collins Street, Melbourne, c. 1900

Sir Redmond Barry, the judge who sentenced Ned Kelly to death, was the principal founder of the Melbourne Public Library, now the State Library of Victoria. Barry dreamed of an antipodean treasure house of books, and a building to match his vision. Joseph Reed, Melbourne's leading architect of the time, won a competition for its design. He produced this classical masterpiece in Palladian style, marked by the columned portico and flanking pavilions. The building was opened in 1856. In 1913, a reading room, with a concrete and glass dome designed by Norman Peebles and engineered by Sir John Monash, was completed. In the photograph, the Corinthian columns have been draped in black in respect for Queen Victoria, who died on 20 January 1901.

Melbourne Public Library, 1901

Until Prince's Bridge was built at Swanston Street in 1850, ferry services punted people and goods across the Yarra River between Melbourne town and the southern settlements. William Watts established the first service in 1838. In South Yarra, the service gave its name to Punt Road, shown here climbing away to the south through the colony's first commercial vineyards. Passengers paid one penny to cross; ox teams crossed on the bridge-like pontoon for sixpence. As the value of land close to the growing city increased, the vineyards were subdivided and the vines transplanted to the Yarra Valley about sixty kilometres north-east of Melbourne. Today, a number of Yarra Valley wines bear the label 'Punt Road Wines'.

Punts at Punt Road, Melbourne, c. 1855

When Governor Macquarie sanctioned the building of a race track on what is now Sydney's Hyde Park in 1810, he did so not only to satisfy the passion of the officers of his 73rd Regiment for horse racing, but also to raise the level of cultural and social life in the colony. For the same reasons, land was set aside at Flemington, just three years after the settlement of Melbourne. Race meetings have always been the scene of important social events in Australia, be they in major cities or humble country towns. This is clearly evident here on the Lawn at Flemington in 1906. The very cream of Melbourne society, at its most chic, is on proud display at the race that 'stops the nation' – the Melbourne Cup.

The Lawn at Flemington, Melbourne, 1906

Lawn Flemington, Melbourne Cup Day.

Judging by their stance and dress, the characters posing here could be two of Melbourne's notorious larrikins, the kind of wild youth the poet CJ Dennis immortalised in his character Ginger Mick. The traffic of the time is no threat to them, nor to the other pedestrians in view. The Royal Mail Hotel is well placed on the corner, Cobb & Co's coach depot being nearby in Bourke Street. In the distance is the Melbourne Town Hall, its clock tower rising above the classical portico. The foundation stone for the town hall was laid by the Duke of Edinburgh in 1867 and the tower named the Prince Alfred Tower in his honour. The portico was added in 1887.

Larrikins in Swanston Street, Melbourne, c. 1890

The long shadows at right angles to the elaborate Italianate facade of the building to the left indicate that it is mid-winter, around midday. The clock on the GPO tower confirms the time. Designed in Neo-Renaissance style, the GPO was built in 1859 to replace an earlier post office building on the site. A third level in Second Empire style, including a mansard-capped tower, was added in 1887. Beyond the far end of Bourke Street can be seen the dim form of St Patrick's Catholic Cathedral, one of the world's last great Gothic cathedrals. Its foundation stone was laid in 1850, but it wasn't completed until 1939 when its central and two forward spires were added.

Bourke Street Looking East, Melbourne, 1870

In 1835, white settlers from Tasmania landed on this wider section of the Yarra River below a stretch of rocky falls, near where William Street is today. Four years later Queen's Wharf had been established on the site, extending the colony's existing port facilities at Williamstown and Sandridge (Port Melbourne). A customs house was established nearby, in a tent. In 1876, the Melbourne Harbour Trust was established to regulate the activities of the bustling port. Here, the photographer has captured the essence of the wharf's activity. In the foreground the angled cables and beams of the crane cut across a vertical tangle of masts and rigging behind, highlighting the function of the wharf – the loading and unloading of cargo.

Unloading Goods, Queen's Wharf, Melbourne, 1875

Surveyor Robert Hoddle is credited with Melbourne's street plan, although there is some doubt about the extent of his contribution. The lanes, midway between the east–west running streets, were included to provide rear access to the lots fronting the main thoroughfares. Each was approximately one-third the width of the broader streets. But the lanes soon took on a residential and commercial life of their own, becoming the 'Little' streets, taking their names from the major thoroughfares to their immediate south. Flinders Lane, however, continued to be called a lane. Here at its western end, substantial warehouses and businesses associated with the nearby wharves were established. Its eastern end became the home of the Melbourne rag trade.

Flinders Lane, Melbourne, 1890

A steam passenger train makes its way along the Flinders Street railway viaduct, snaking its way towards Spencer Street Station (now Southern Cross) past busy Queen's Wharf, just below the Queen Street Bridge. Wharves and warehouses also line the Yarra's southern bank. The passenger rolling stock is parked on the roof of vaulted commercial premises built as part of the viaduct project, and now known as Banana Alley. Along Flinders Street, the tracks of Melbourne's cable tram system can just be made out. The slender street poles with their multiple crossbars carry the city's telecommunication lines. It's a vibrant scene that captures the infrastructures of thriving late nineteenth century Melbourne.

The Yarra Below Queen's Bridge, Melbourne, c. 1895

Proud and confident of its burgeoning manufacturing and agricultural industries, in 1866 Melbourne staged an Inter-Colonial Exhibition. A Great Hall was built in Swanston Street to house the exhibition behind the Melbourne Public Library, now the State Library of Victoria. The Machinery Room, shown here, contains numerous examples of the technical inventiveness and manufacturing prowess that was to make Melbourne the manufacturing capital of Australia. Art was not forgotten. Note the plaster replica of the Elgin Marbles decorating the upper walls of the hall. The Great Hall became part of the Melbourne Museum. In 2000, the museum was moved into a new building sited beside Melbourne's world heritage–listed Royal Exhibition Building, which was originally constructed for the International Exhibition of 1880.

Machinery Room of the Inter-Colonial Exhibition, Melbourne, 1866–67

London architects JW Fawcett and MP Ashworth designed Melbourne's Flinders Street Station. Their brief was to design a building on the corner of Flinders and Swanston streets that would provide a focal point for the city. The result is Melbourne's Edwardian Baroque masterpiece. The contract was let in 1905, and work completed in 1910. Here, shown under construction, is the grand clock tower above the northern facade that extends more than a city block to the west along Flinders Street. The tower addresses the full length of Elizabeth Street, providing a commanding focal point for it. The intersection was the terminus for the busy northern cable-tram line. Today, the intersection is still a busy transit point for train and tram passengers.

Constructing Flinders Street Station, Melbourne, 1909

Since the gold rushes of the 1850s, Victoria has had a vibrant Chinese community. In Melbourne, it was concentrated in Little Bourke Street's China Town, and still is. Here, in Spring Street, a Chinese procession celebrates the opening of the new Commonwealth Parliament in 1901. The partially revealed building on the left is Victoria's State Parliament House, designed by architect Peter Kerr in the Roman Revival style. It became the seat of the federal government until Canberra's Parliament House was completed in 1927. The building to the distant right is the Melbourne Treasury, an outstanding example of Neo-Renaissance style. It was designed by nineteen-year-old public works draughtsman JJ Clark.

Chinese Procession, Melbourne, 1901

This tranquil scene, reminiscent of rural England, is the work of the university architect, Joseph Reed, Melbourne's most prolific architect of its great growth period in the nineteenth century. Reed produced a large range of building types in a variety of revivalist styles. His works include the Melbourne Public Library, the Melbourne Town Hall, and the Independent Church in Collins Street. The facade of his Neo-Renaissance Bank of New South Wales in Collins Street was re-erected in the university when the bank was demolished in the 1960s. Cathedral-like Wilson Hall, shown here from the rear, was a gem in rustic Gothic style. It was destroyed by fire in 1952. The castellated building to its right is the Arts Building, now known as the Old Arts Building.

University of Melbourne, 1880s

elbourne was the first Australian city to install an electric power generator, shown here being installed in Lonsdale Street. It was called the City of Melbourne Electric Lighting Station. One year later, electric lighting had replaced the gas lamps in Melbourne streets. In 1906, building of the infrastructure for municipal electric tramway systems was begun. The systems were powered by private electric companies. Electrification of the cable tram network began in 1924, and was completed in 1940. In 1913 the first electric train service ran from Flinders Street to Essendon, and soon after to the Melbourne Showgrounds and the Flemington Racecourse. The electrification of the entire suburban rail network quickly followed.

Installing Melbourne's Electric Generator, 1893

— WORKING LIFE —

*A nation doesn't emerge from a cluster of settler colonies
without hard work, toil on the land, and work in the towns and cities.
For many it was hard yakka, for some it was less taxing.
For most, it was a struggle.*

It's small wonder that working people celebrated the Eight Hour Day, given that before the award was granted many worked twelve to sixteen hours a day, six days a week. Victorian stonemasons led the way with a street protest on 21 April 1856 when thousands marched through the city streets under the banners of the various trade unions. The Victorian government made this day a public holiday in 1879. It was renamed Labour Day in 1934 and moved to the first Monday in March. The last procession in Melbourne was in 1951. In 1955, the Moomba Festival Parade took its place.

Eight Hour Day Celebration, Melbourne, c. 1900

This is the kind of scene the poet Banjo Paterson might have envisaged when he created Clancy, the character of his famous poem 'Clancy of the Overflow'. Here the real 'Clancys' take a break while their cattle feed on a lush 'long paddock', although the number of dead trees suggests that a recent drought has taken its toll. The long paddock was the name given to a designated travelling stock route. Boundary fences, where they existed, were set well back from the stock routes to create wide verges that drovers could exploit for grazing. Droving in Queensland, and northern Australia generally, provided employment for many young Aboriginal men who were able to put to good use their remarkable prowess on horseback.

Drovers in Queensland, 1880s

This picture represents a dark era in the history of Queensland. The women shown hoeing the cane field are Kanakas (Hawaiian for 'boys'). Kanakas were indentured labour brought to Australia from the Pacific islands to work on cane and cotton plantations. The practice was begun by sea captain Robert Towns, who imported sixty-seven workers in 1867 to work for a pittance on his cotton plantation. As the practice became more widespread it became akin to slavery. Shipmasters known as 'blackbirders' roved the Pacific islands to gather up workers, often using deception, coercion, and even kidnapping. The practice was finally outlawed by the Australian government, following Federation in 1901. The Queensland town Townsville is named after Captain Towns.

Kanaka Women, Queensland, 1890s

KANAKA WOMEN WORKING IN SUGAR CANE

The Gundagai theatre is primitive by contemporary standards, but no doubt advances in antiseptic practices had been made on earlier times. The lack of breathing masks and the exposed hair of the nurses indicates, however, that there is still some way to go. Improved hygiene and patient care were introduced into Australian hospitals by English nurse Lucy Osborne in 1867. Osborne had trained at the Florence Nightingale College of Nursing in London, and was invited by New South Wales' Premier Henry Parkes to run the Sydney Infirmary and Dispensary. The anaesthetist here is using chloroform applied to a cloth wad placed over the patient's nose and mouth, a distressing, suffocating experience. She stands at the ready should the patient wake prematurely.

Operating Theatre, Gundagai, New South Wales, c. 1900

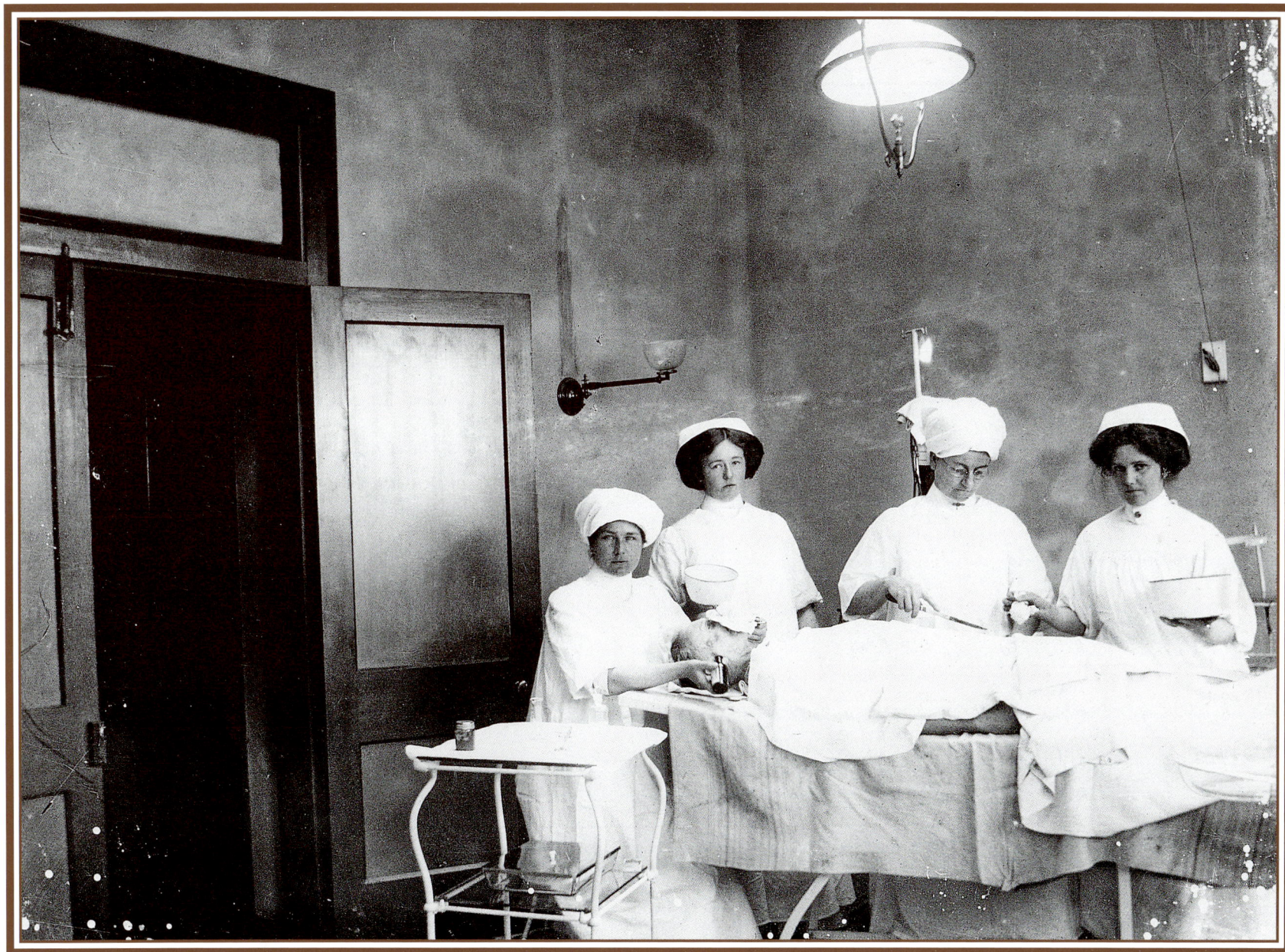

*I*t may not have been hard work, but it certainly must have been tedious. We can only hope these young women were not packing Life Savers all day, every day. The popular lolly was produced by MacRobertson's Chocolates, the company that gave us the Freddo Frog and Cherry Ripe. From first producing sweets in his mother's converted bathroom, George MacPherson Robertson rose to become Australia's 'chocolate king'. By the 1920s he was Australia's wealthiest man. He was also one of Melbourne's leading philanthropists. He endowed the MacRobertson Girls' High School and the Emily MacPherson College for women, and financed the elegant MacRobertson Bridge that links Toorak with Burnley across the Yarra River. He died in 1945. His company was bought out by Cadburys in 1967.

Packing Life Savers, Fitzroy, Melbourne, c. 1920

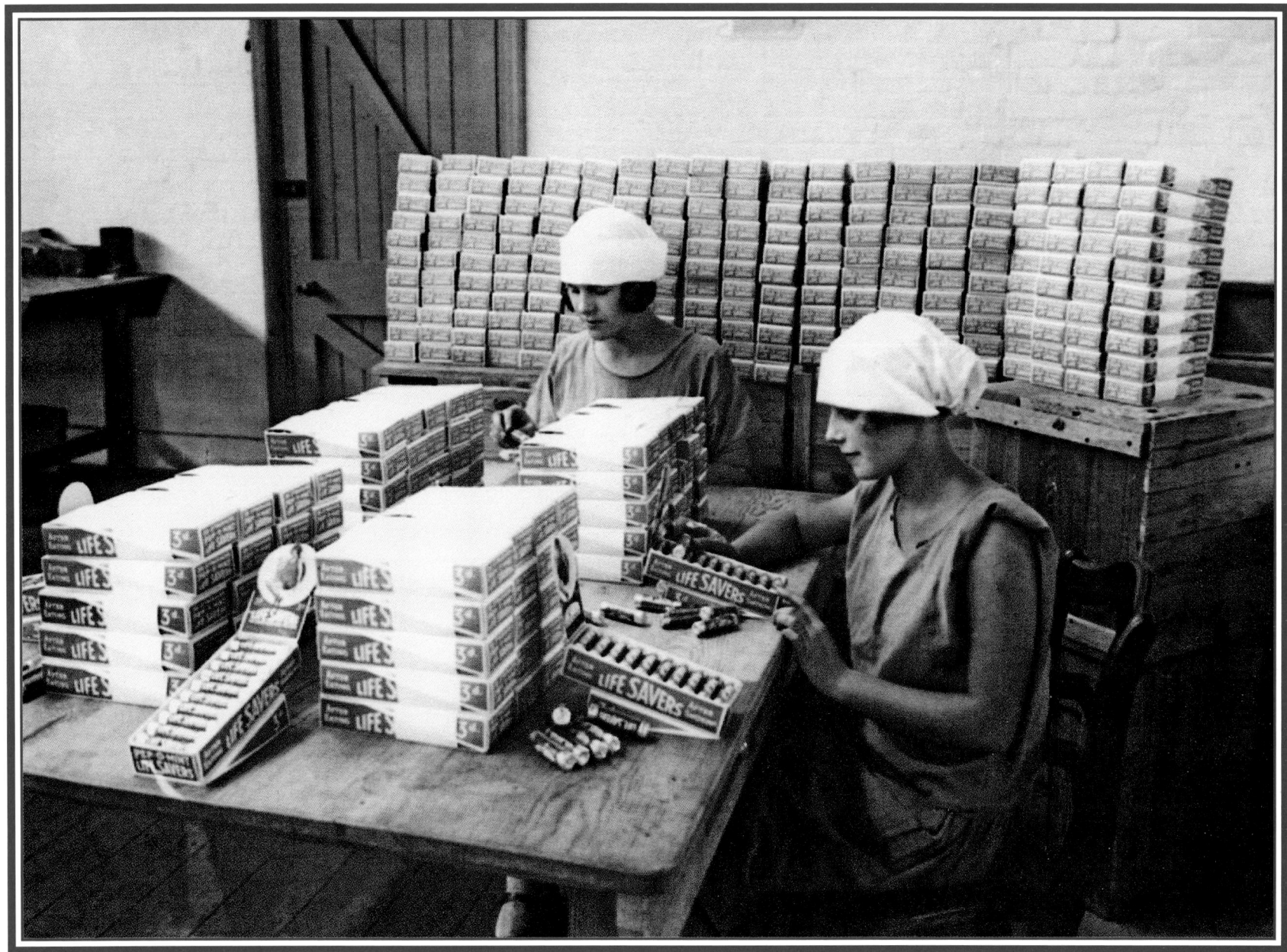

Thomas Johnson appears to have had an affinity with ancient Rome. The original Pantheon houses the tombs of ancient Rome's greats, and the facade of Johnson's impressive factory is in the Romanesque style. But the activity inside the building was anything but grand. The men and women photographed here worked long hours for low wages in appalling conditions. Cutters worked, heads down, all day to make their daily quotas. 'Closers' sewed the uppers; others worked at machines sewing uppers to soles; others at 'clicker' machines punching lace-holes. And all amid the constant clatter and heat generated by the machines. Small wonder that there was industrial trouble at Johnson's factories in 1874. The bootmaking industry has now all but vanished from the Australian industrial scene.

Johnson's Pantheon Boot Factory, Adelaide, c. 1872

*T*his group of streetsweepers are the descendants of Sydney's 'blockboys', so called because the streets they swept in an earlier age were paved with wooden blocks. The blockboys, also known as 'sparrow starvers', kept the streets clear of horse dung and other litter. Employed by the council, many started at age fourteen. By 1937, despite the advent of the motor car, there were still many horse-drawn vehicles plying Sydney streets. And, of course, there were no motorised mechanical streetsweepers then. So, what with horse dung and general litter, there was plenty of work for a man with a broom. Perhaps this band is smiling because they hold a secure job during the years of the Great Depression.

Sydney Streetsweepers, 1937

What skill these tree fellers have! The coordination and balance required to axe the wedge-cut into this forest giant from those narrow springboards is breathtaking. And there are the skills we don't see – the cross-cut sawing from the opposite side, and the driving in of wedges to effect an accurate fall to the forest floor. West Gippsland's dense forests of mountain ash provided a rich supply of timber for early Victoria. Forests were cleared for farming, and the timber that wasn't burnt was cut into railway sleepers and woodblocks to pave Melbourne's streets. In the nineteenth century, inefficient drying techniques constrained the timber for the building industry, but it took off after World War I with the development of kiln- and steam-drying methods of seasoning.

Tree Felling, Morwell, Victoria, 1913

Until the 1970s, work for most young women was regarded as a gap period, filling the time between school and marriage. Many went directly into factories, others became shop assistants. Some prepared for the offices of the commercial world by taking courses in business colleges. There they learnt typing, shorthand and elementary bookkeeping. The best of them became secretaries, taking dictation, typing letters and reports, answering the phone, and managing the diaries of their bosses. Some, no doubt, were more intelligent than the men they worked for. And, of course, their rates of pay were much less than those for men. The dress and posture of the women pictured here was part of their training, designed to give style to an office and dignity to their work.

Typing Class, 1937

So impressed was champion billiards player Walter Lindrum by the quality of the Mintaro slate used in billard table construction, he wrote, in 1931, to congratulate the quarry. Mined almost continuously at Mintaro since 1856, the slate has always been regarded as one of the finest in the world. Here, in 1873, it was naturally exposed, making extraction and hand-splitting relatively easy. In colonial times it was used extensively as a roofing material in the building of houses, churches, and public and commercial buildings. It still is a much-prized finishing material. Its smooth, velvety surfaces make excellent paving for flat surfaces indoors and out, as well as for steps and vertical edgings.

Mintaro Slate Quarry, South Australia, 1872

The men here are working on a section of a concrete channel system in north-central South Australia. The channel was built to take water from the Broughton River to irrigate broad-acre farming in the Jamestown area. A dam at Bundaleer was part of the system. Five hundred men worked on the dam and twenty-six kilometres of channel. A town was built for the workers, replete with shops, a post office and a police station. It even had a cricket team. The nature of the work limited the use of horses, so much of the work carving out the channel and building the embankments was done by men toiling with picks, shovels and wheelbarrows. And yet the project, begun in 1898, was completed in 1902.

Water Channel at Bundaleer, South Australia, 1898

The shearers here are using machine-driven shears, rather than hand-operated blade cutters. Irish immigrant and inventor Frederick York Wolseley developed the machine on his Euroka station in New South Wales over an eleven year period, from 1877 to 1888. Despite early resistance from shearers, the higher daily tallies, larger fleeces and reduced injuries to sheep convinced both shearers and bosses alike that the machine-driven system was a winner. By 1890 the machines were in general use. They certainly reduced wrist strain, but did nothing for the shearer's back. He had to wait for the body-supporting sling to reduce back strain. Wolseley established a company to manufacture his machines in Birmingham, UK. His engineer partner, Herbert Austin, went on to develop the Austin Wolseley motor car.

Machine Shearing, Victoria, c. 1890

This is the kind of quarry that produced the stone for early Tasmania's public buildings and bridges, and the houses of the wealthy. The photograph dramatises well the primitive methods of extraction used at the time. The men appear overwhelmed by the mass and weight of the granite they work. And yet they succeed, using chisels, wedges and sledgehammers to split the stone, first from the rock face and then into manageable blocks. Crowbars and levers are used to manipulate the blocks into positions where they can be winched to level, clear ground. The worker on the left has driven a series of chisels into a block that will, with further sledging, split the block in two.

Stone Quarry, Tasmania, c. 1895

*M*aster photographer Frank Hurley has used the giant O ring, and the light from the clerestory window, to great dramatic effect, capturing the grime, the apparent confusion and even the heat of the shop floor of BHP's Newcastle steelworks. BHP, incorporated in 1888, expanded its Broken Hill metals operations into steel production at Newscastle in 1915. Its first blast furnace had an annual capacity of 150,000 tons of steel. In 1917 the company formed a shipping fleet to transport iron ore from Iron Knob in South Australia to the steelworks in New South Wales. By 1943 it had ten 'Iron ships'. During World War II it lost the *Iron Chiefton* and the *Iron Knight* to Japanese submarine attacks in Australian coastal waters.

Newcastle Steelworks, New South Wales, c. 1920

— COUNTRY LIFE —

A settler society, by its nature, creates a life on the land for farmers, pastoralists and, in Australia's case, gold seekers. Cities develop around ports, but towns, large and small, spring up to serve directly the surrounding life in the country.

This scene brings to mind Henry Lawson's short story 'The Drover's Wife'. The dense bush looming behind the cottage highlights the settlers' isolation; the absence of the father emphasises the aloneness and vulnerability of the woman and her children. Happily, though, the jinker may indicate occasional visits to neighbours and the nearest town. She and her children appear to have dressed in their Sunday best for the photographer, although it hasn't extended to shoes for the children. The stumps of felled trees set against the towering forest tell us something of the toil involved in carving out this tiny holding.

Settler's Wife and Children, c. 1890

A PIONEER SETTLER

The word 'overlanders' was first used to describe those who drove sheep from New South Wales to the new colony of South Australia in 1838. But it wasn't the first livestock drive in Australian history. Sheep had been driven from New South Wales to the Port Phillip District earlier in the decade. For those first overlanders, there were no stock routes through the bush; they moved through what to them was virgin territory. However, the presence of the dray in the camp pictured here indicates that this crew trekked along known tracks. The cook was an indispensable member of the crew, often travelling ahead of the mob to set up camp and prepare for tired, hungry drovers. Here, in the morning, they enjoy his coffee.

Overlanders' Camp, 1900

OVERLANDERS (A...
(MORNING COFFEE.)

The electric street poles date this scene in the early twentieth century. The proprietors stand proudly before their store with its upper-level dwelling. Their shop is chock-full of goods to supply the town and surrounding area. Picton, south-west of Sydney, is located in an area that was known in colonial times as the Cowspastures, so named because cattle that had escaped there from the settlement at Sydney Cove in 1788 were left to roam free and breed. John Macarthur, father of the Australian wool industry, took up land in the area to establish Camden. In 1819, Governor Macquarie built the Great Southern Road (now the Hume Highway) through the region, and a later road from Camden further opened up the area. The town was originally called Stonequarry.

General Store, Picton, New South Wales, c. 1930s

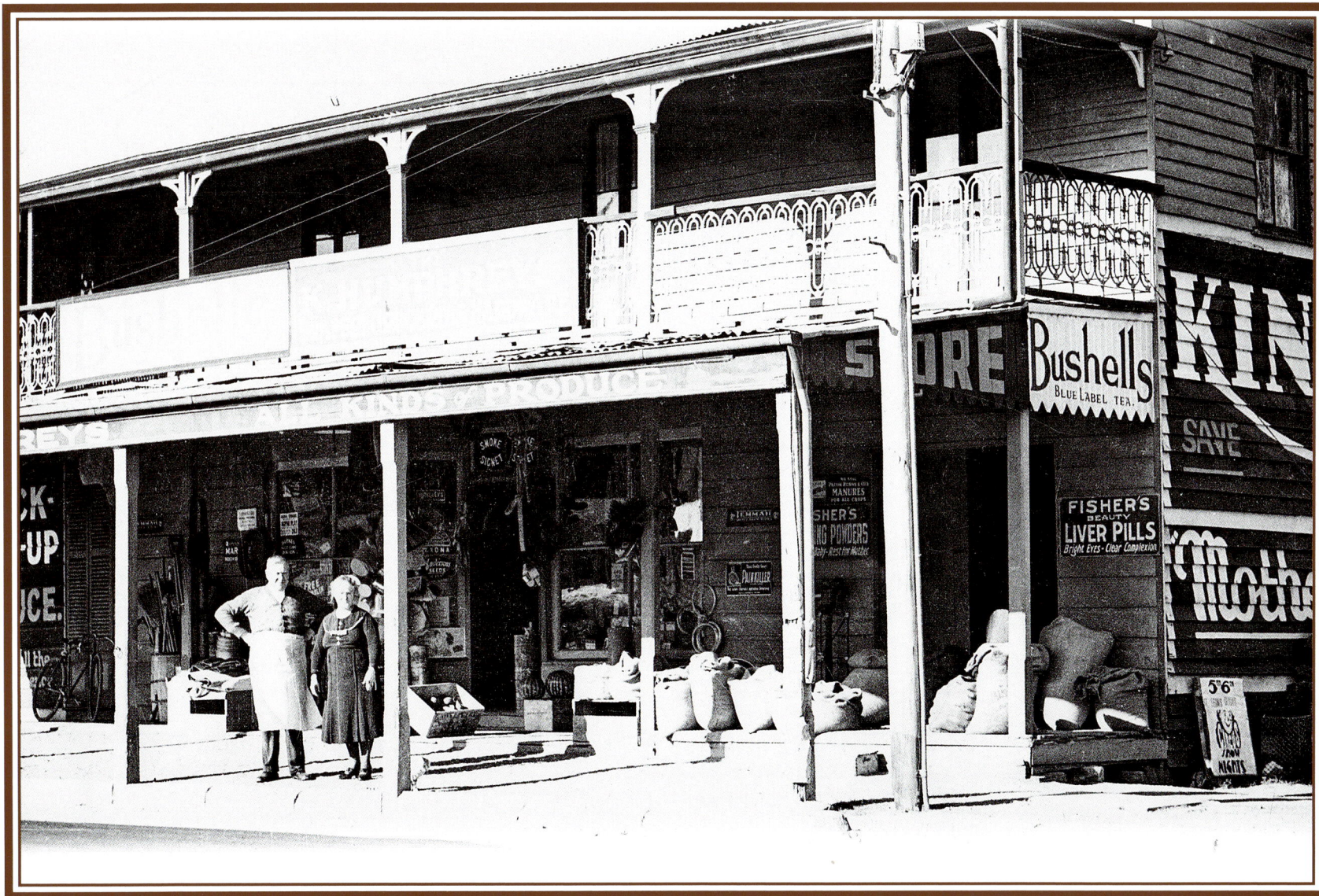

Wood splitters cut and shaped felled timber into railway sleepers, palings, and fence posts and rails. Their tools were the cross-cut saw, the splitter, the adze for shaping, and the popular curve-sided Kelly axe, considered by R Kaleski, in his *Australian Complete Settlers' Guide* (1909), to be 'the best all-round axe'. The life of the splitters was isolated and tough; the shotgun tells us they would have supplemented their salted meat rations with fresh rabbit meat when they could. The fruit of their work is all around them. The walls of their hut are split palings, and its bark roof is anchored by timber they have rejected. The post-and-rail bush fence running behind the hut is also the work of splitters.

Wood Splitters near Lilydale, Victoria, c. 1890

Swagmen, 'swaggies', were a common sight in the Australian bush during the nineteenth and early twentieth centuries. Itinerant workers, they walked the bush in search of work, carrying their meagre belongings wrapped in a blanket called a swag, often called a 'bluey' because it was usually blue. 'Humping the bluey' was how their life was often described. The two here, leaning confidently on their walking sticks, topped with rams' horns, appear undefeated by the life they lead. Perhaps the rifle bolsters the confidence of the man on the left. In drought and depression years, though, swaggies suffered terribly. The spivvy-looking bloke, perhaps a townsman and mate, appears more than happy to be photographed with them. Poet Banjo Paterson immortalised the swagman in his song 'Waltzing Matilda'.

Swagmen, Gundagai, New South Wales, c. 1910

ife on the farm was a family affair. Children, many old before their time, worked hard when they weren't at school. Writer Edward Sorenson, drawing on his first-hand experience of bush life, said of bush children they were 'hard worked ... [their] knowledge is of cattle and horses, of reptiles, beetles, birds and animals, and their home and playground the trackless bush' (*Life in the Australian Backblocks*). Here, the older boy has harnessed up a bullock team of poddy calves to drag the milk cans down to the front gate ready for the milk truck. The little fellow on the sled leans on a milk can in the manner of his father leaning on a gate, or fence post.

Children on the Farm, c. 1900

In 1836, squatter Thomas Kite established his Burrawang Run on land across the Blue Mountains, west of Sydney. By 1866, his sheep run, now a 'station', covered approximately 217,000 hectares of rich pasture land. In 1884, wool production at the station reached a record 5000 bales. Two hundred and fifty men worked the shearing sheds, sheds that contained 101 shearing stands. The photograph reveals the hive of activity that surrounded the skirting tables, where men trimmed the ragged and sweaty edges, the dags and the belly wool from the fleeces. Wool classers then removed the inferior fleeces, the 'casts', and graded the wool before it was sent to the pressers to be baled in jute bags. Wool classing was the most respected job in the shearing shed.

Wool Sorting at Burrawang Station, New South Wales, 1899

Originally, gold attracted Europeans to the Kinglake area. A settlement sprang up in 1861 at Mountain Rush close to the present town. When the gold petered out, timber cutters moved in to supply Melbourne's increasing demand for timber. Horse and bullock teams dragged the timber to the railhead at Whittlesea. In the early1900s an extensive network of tramways replaced the draught animals. By the 1920s, the timber industry was giving way to potato and berry fruit farming. These workers pose at their sawmill during the transition period. A national park was established in 1928 to preserve what was left of the forests. The town has no lake. It was named after the internationally renowned author Alexander Kinglake, despite the fact that he had never visited the town.

Timber Workers at Kinglake, Victoria, c. 1920

The Kurrajong area in the Hawkesbury Valley north-west of Sydney is rich, fertile farming country. Emancipated convict Joseph Douglass took up a land grant there in 1825, the first European to do so. One hundred years later, the New South Wales government established forty-six soldier settler scheme blocks there for returned World War I diggers. In such a mixed farming area, haymaking was an annual, seasonal event. Here local farmers join forces to build a stack. The lifting contraption works on the lever principle. Horsepower raises and lowers it, while a device swivels it across to be pitchforked onto the growing stack. The farm dog, for some reason, looks wary. 'Kurrajong' was an Aboriginal name for a tree, the bark of which was used for making twine.

Building a Haystack at Kurrajong, New South Wales, 1937

The itinerant knife sharpener was a familiar sight in country towns and on bush roads in the nineteenth century. His services were sought by housewives, tradesmen, and beardless men needing to keep their cut-throats razor sharp. It's not surprising that he has set up here outside the local tailor's shop. He's also well placed for an ale when he finishes work; his dog waits patiently, in the shade. The town of Forbes has a rich gold rush and bushranging history. It was at the heart of the territory ranged by the notorious Ben Hall. And Australia's richest gold robbery occurred on the road from Forbes to Bathurst when Frank Gardiner and a gang of seven held up the gold escort coach in 1862.

Itinerant Knife Sharpener, Forbes, New South Wales, c. 1890

*J*ust about every country town in nineteenth- and early-twentieth-century Australia had its blacksmith's shop. Which is to be expected, given that the horse was the principal means of power on the farm and road, not to mention the versatile role of the farm hack. And, as most districts had their race track, racing gave the blacksmith work, too. He made and fitted horseshoes, forged and fitted the steel rims of cartwheels, and did metal-work repairs on farms. Whittlesea, fifty kilometres north of Melbourne, was a railhead where timber, wool and other farm products were hauled by horse and bullock teams for shipment to Melbourne. It's not surprising that the local blacksmith had plenty of work.

Blacksmith's Shop, Whittlesea, Victoria, c. 1885

Washing took up a full day in the working week of a settler's wife. If proof were needed of how hard these pioneer women worked, it is here. She lit and stoked the fire, and then, over the heat of the boiling water, agitated the wash with her copper stick. Using the stick again, she transferred the heavy, dripping mass to the cold-water tub, lifting and plunging to rinse. Hand-wringing and then folding the wash into those neat skeins no doubt took their toll on her wrists. And there's not a machine in sight, except for the makeshift flying fox her ingenious husband has rigged up to bring water from a tank nearby. Finally, she had to get it dry, a drawn-out chore in wet weather.

Washing Day, Lake Tyers, Victoria, c. 1900

In 1872, Henry Beaufoy Merlin of the American and Australasian Photographic Company produced a series of photographs recording life in the towns of Hill End and Gulgong, New South Wales. His pictures combined houses with portraits of their occupants. Here, at Hill End, in this carefully crafted composition, a mother and daughter pose in their Sunday-best clothes. Their attire, though, doesn't hide the realities of their life. The crude little cottage is wattle and daub, the bark roof is anchored with sapling, and there's no room for the wash tubs and buckets inside. But the highly polished chair might well have been, along with her fine clothing, a hedge against the harsh conditions of her life. On the other hand, it could have been a studio prop.

Mother and Daughter, Hill End, New South Wales, 1872

In the days before the mass production of clothing, the tailor was an indispensable tradesman in every country town. Men, women and children need clothing. Mr Kennedy's board shows he is proud of his Sydney origins, suggesting the townsfolk needn't go to the big city to get the best. Perhaps he left Sydney in search of a fortune in gold at Hill End, but like many diggers was forced to revert to his trade. No doubt he's getting by, but his primitive wattle-and-daub shop, with its bark roof, suggests he has some way to go before he makes his fortune. He appears not successful enough yet to need an apprentice; perhaps the cocky kid beside him is his son.

Practical Tailor, Hill End, New South Wales, 1872

J. KENNEDY
PRACTICAL TAILOR
LATE OF SYDNEY.

MAKING TRACKS

The nineteenth and early twentieth centuries saw huge advances in both private and public transport throughout Australia: horse-drawn buses and trams gave way first to cable and then to electric power; the steam train replaced the coach, the bullock train and the lorry. And the invention of the safety bicycle and motor car revolutionised private transport.

Velocipede, from the Latin for 'swift foot', was the name given to the earliest forms of pedal-powered human locomotion. Prior to the invention of the 'safety bicycle' in 1885, there were numerous versions of the machine – two-, three- and four-wheelers – all designed to enable the rider to 'walk fast'. The tricycle version shown here has a complicated pedal, sprocket and chain mechanism driving the front axle. The steering bar and its stem turns the entire front section, limiting manoeuvrability. And there's no sign of a brake. The mudguard on the rear wheel is a nice touch, protecting this man-about-town's spiffy attire from thrown-up dust and gravel, or worse.

Tricycle, 1880s

To encourage closer settlement and more intensive farming, in the 1860s the colonial governments of Victoria and News South Wales passed land acts allowing colonists to select small parcels of land. Many 'selectors' failed because of the harsh bush conditions, and because the best land had often been tied up by the wealthy 'squatters'. Perhaps the family here are selectors on the move to take up a piece of land, or perhaps they're leaving their farm, defeated, after a long battle with drought. Judging by their forlorn expressions it would appear to be the latter. Whichever, they are the bush poor, the kind of people Henry Lawson wrote stories about. What better way to move the bullock than to team it up with the horse.

Bush Family on the Move, c. 1870

What better way to transport the family to the work picnic than by covered phaeton, if you are well-to-do enough to own one and the horses to draw it. Here, at the annual picnic of Adelaide manufacturers 'Alec Simpson and Sons', the Simpson family poses for the camera whilst enjoying their picnic in front of the family carriage. As you might expect, their four-wheeler is the grandest there. Note the side curtains that provide privacy and protection against the weather, and the stylish Art Nouveau detailing of the back rests of the seats, particularly the front. The inward-facing rear seats would have allowed the young people to enjoy each other's company to the maximum during the ride.

Family Picnic in the Phaeton, 1899

The 'ordinary' bicycle, nicknamed the penny-farthing, was invented in the 1870s. It was so named because it resembled an English penny and farthing placed side by side. The front wheel was large to facilitate speed. Its radius was approximated to the length of a man's leg, and the pedals were connected directly to the axle. The high seat meant doing a 'header', or coming a 'cropper', was on the cards. Mounting was tricky, a small peg attached low to the rear axle the only aid. Dismounting was difficult, too. To brake, the rider applied backward pressure on the pedals. So, getting around on a penny-farthing was only for the skilful, the fit and the agile, like the young enthusiasts posing for the camera here.

Penny-Farthing Club, c. 1880s

You would think this family, all three generations of them, would have much to smile about, having just arrived at a hotel in their spic-'n'-span coupe landau, replete with their liveried footman, standing out of frame. On the other hand, perhaps they are glum because they are leaving. This is how the Australian 'aristocracy' got about. Their clothing indicates their class, too. The landau, named after the German city where it was first produced, was the 'crème de la crème' of horse-drawn carriages. Lightweight and suspended over four wheels on elliptical springs, it was convertible, having a soft folding top. Its two facing seats, with a dropped footwell, facilitated conversation. The swept, curved base gave it an elegant profile, enhanced here by the fine line work of the coach painter.

Family in a Landau, 1880s

Chaperoned by the lady on the left, these girls are about to enjoy the pleasures of the cycling craze that swept Australia in the late 1880s, a craze facilitated by the invention of the safety bicycle in 1885. The new bicycle, with two wheels of equal diameter, the rear being driven by a pedal and chain mechanism, was much safer than the penny-farthing. The girls here don't appear to be wearing bloomers, those ballooning trousers that were to make cycling more convenient for a woman, if she were daring enough to wear them in public. By the end of the century, the new bicycle had made cycling a common means of 'getting around' for men and women, the young and not-so-young.

The Cycling Party, Adelaide, 1896

The horse-drawn tram was a natural and desirable extension of the horse bus, given that city streets could become potholed and rutted. Rails smoothed out what could otherwise be a rocky ride. Sydney experimented briefly with horse trams in 1861, but the engineers didn't sink the rails into the road surface, leaving a hazard for other traffic. The city then adopted steam-powered trams before the advent of electrification. Brisbane and Adelaide installed extensive horse-tram networks; Melbourne adopted the cable system. Here, in what appears to be Adelaide's King William Street, well-dressed gentlemen are happy to travel on the city's double-deckers, the last of which was taken out of service in 1914. By then, electricity had replaced horse power.

Horse Trams, Adelaide, 1909

Design is always evolutionary. Take a coupe phaeton, remove the shafts and other equine equipment, then reconfigure the seats, install a steam engine and steering mechanism, and you have a steam automobile. That's what Melbourne engineer Herbert Thomson did at his Armadale workshop, and he called it a 'six-seat phaeton'. Thomson presented his steam car to the public in 1899. In April 1890 he drove it from Bathurst, New South Wales, to Melbourne, a distance of 794 kilometres, at an average speed of fourteen kilometres per hour. The car had a two-speed gearing system. Unfortunately, it had to be stopped to change gears. Using a screwdriver, the driver had to prise a drive belt from one pulley to another. Thomson made twelve cars, but couldn't compete with the new imported petrol-driven cars.

Thomson's Steam Car, Melbourne, c. 1899

Melbourne's cable tram system was one of the most extensive in the world. It consisted of a network of double tracks along seventeen routes radiating a total distance of seventy-five kilometres from the city into the suburbs. Twelve hundred trams made up the fleet. Traction was by a continuously moving cable accessible through a continuous slot beneath the road surface midway between the rails. The tram had a mechanism for gripping and disengaging the cable. The driver was called the 'gripman'. In dual cars, he operated from a front, open car, called the 'dummy'. But, as the photograph shows, there were other, less mechanical ways of getting about Melbourne streets in the 1890s. The last cable service was discontinued in 1940. Note the hardwood blocks paving the street.

Cable Trams in Melbourne's Collins Street, c. 1890

MELBOURNE. COLLINS St NEAR QUEEN St.

Built in 1878, the *Ruby* carried cargo and passengers along what was then called Australia's 'water highway', the Murray-Darling river system. In 1908, she was converted to a barge and renamed the *Radia*, and replaced by a new *Ruby*, Here is the original vessel in her heyday during a pleasure cruise along the Murray, her passengers enjoying a short interlude on the banks of the mighty river. Paddle-steamers carried supply goods into the remote pastoral properties of inland Australia, and returned to ports and railheads along the river laden with the wool that made Australia rich. The new *Ruby* operated until 1938. From that time she lay moored and rotting wharfside at Wentworth, until restored by enthusiasts in 2007.

Paddle-steamer Ruby, New South Wales, c. 1900

This lady could do with a helping hand from the gentleman behind her. She's boarding a Standard Combination electric tram in the Government Precinct, William Street, Brisbane. The city changed directly from its original horse-drawn trams to electric power, having rejected the cable system as unsuitable for the Brisbane terrain. Standard Combination trams were introduced in 1897. Before then a number of horse trams had been converted to electric power. The new trams, commonly known as the 'matchboxes', were purpose-built for the new electric system. Sixty-three were constructed between 1897 and 1904. Most had a two-man crew, a driver and conductor. Some that travelled the short routes had just the driver. The last was taken out of service in 1952.

Lady Boards Electric Tram, Brisbane, c. 1910

There were enough owners of automobiles in Melbourne in 1903 to form a motoring club – the Royal Automobile Club of Victoria (RACV). It was formed initially as a social club to provide facilities and organise rallies for its members. The first rally, in July 1903, was to Aspendale Park Race Course on Port Phillip Bay, twenty-five kilometres south of Melbourne. The second, shown here, was to Marysville in the Great Dividing Range, eighty kilometres north-east of Melbourne. Everything is in good style: the chauffeurs are liveried, the owner-drivers wear the customary cap and dust coat, while the ladies wear their elegant Edwardian attire. Note the adventurous lady driver in the car third from the left.

RACV Outing, Marysville, Victoria, 1904

All six Australian colonial governments constructed railways during the great railway age of the second half of the nineteenth century. Two principal factors governed the extent of the networks they built – geography and wealth. Victoria, for example, a small colony and the richest, developed extensive country and metropolitan networks. South Australia, by contrast, developed far fewer services. It built its first line, from Adelaide to Port Adelaide, in 1856, but later in the century invested mainly in tram and trolley bus passenger systems. One notable exception was the privately owned train service from Glenelg to King William Street, Adelaide. Here, on the morning the service ceased to operate, business men disperse from the terminus to their various places of work in the city centre.

The Glenelg Train, Adelaide, South Australia, 1914

166

— RECREATION AND SPORTING LIFE —

When the British colonised Australia in the late eighteenth century it was only natural that they would bring with them the games, organised sports and other leisure activities they had enjoyed in the home country.

The early settlers of South Australia were determined to make the colony the 'Britannia of the Antipodes'. Fox hunting was as British a pastime as one could be, so it wasn't surprising that the Adelaide Hunt Club was formed in 1840, just four years after British settlement. The scene here could be one of aristocratic England, save for the crudeness of the colonial architecture and grounds, and the eucalyptus trees. Members of a local club have gathered ready for the chase, replete with livery, horse and hound. And the occasion doesn't lack an enthusiastic audience either: gentlemen look on, and family members take advantage of the balcony to overlook the departure. Woodville, a preferred suburb of the wealthy, was one of the first areas to be settled outside Adelaide town.

Hunting at Woodville, South Australia, 1870

Croquet was a popular recreation in colonial Australia, for a number of reasons. First and probably foremost, it was an outdoor game that allowed women and men to compete on equal terms. Second, it could be played anywhere, provided a level patch of ground could be found, even roughly level, as here. And all that was needed were the hoops, mallets and balls; no special clothing was required. Angaston, in the Barossa Valley, is not far from Kapunda where, in 1887, the first croquet club in South Australia was formed. One year earlier, the first Australian club was established at Kyneton, Victoria. From these beginnings, the croquet club lawns of today developed.

Croquet at Angaston, 1867

Australia's most famous Aboriginal cricketer was demon fast bowler Eddie Gilbert. Gilbert played for Queensland in the Sheffield Shield Competition, and against visiting touring teams. He bowled Sir Donald Bradman out twice in Shield matches. However, he never played for Australia. Some believe it was because he was black, for others it was because his bowling action was suspect, despite slow-motion cameras finding no fault with it. The first Australian cricket team to tour England was all-Aboriginal. It toured in 1868, winning as many games as it lost. Shown here are Aboriginal men of the Yarra tribes who were forced to live on reserved land at Coranderk (now Healesville) sixty kilometres north-east of Melbourne. They farmed the land, and made and traded Aboriginal artefacts. And they enjoyed playing cricket!

Cricket Match at Coranderk, Victoria, 1887

Lake Wendouree was the centre of nineteenth century Ballarat's recreational life. Gentlemen and ladies promenaded along its six-kilometre encircling path. Boat houses dotted its shores, some home to boat-hiring businesses like the one shown here. Yachties, canoeists and rowers enjoyed its tranquil, safe waters. Gardens surrounded it, kiosks and tea rooms provided refreshments, and small paddle-steamers (fifteen in the 1860s) ferried passengers across to the Ballarat Botanical Gardens. In 1851, the lake was dammed to provide the thriving town with a water supply, and in 1864 a rowing course was cut through its weedy centre. In 1956 it hosted the rowing and canoeing events of the Melbourne Olympics.

Lake Wendouree, Ballarat, Victoria, 1880s

Emulating England's Henley Regatta on the Thames, Melbourne's Henley-on-Yarra was a high point of pleasure and excitement in Melbourne's social calendar. It was certainly a place for the fashionable 'to be seen'. Held on the Saturday before the Melbourne Cup, it attracted huge crowds. In 1925, 300,000 people attended. Boating in all kinds of small craft attracted the young, and the not-so-young. Fine food and drink were dispensed from the numerous pavilions lining the river banks. But for many, the main attraction was the boat racing. Henley was the principal still-water boat racing day of the year. The Regatta, inaugurated in 1905, was discontinued soon after World War II.

Henley-on-Yarra, Melbourne, 1909

From their inception in the early twentieth century, international tennis competitions were major sporting and social events of the Australian scene, as they still are. The Davis Cup competition between England and the United States was inaugurated in 1900. When the competition was expanded, Australia, in partnership with New Zealand, soon made a challenge. After two unsuccessful attempts, Norman Brookes and Kiwi Anthony Wilding wrested the cup from the powerful Americans in 1907. The American challenge of 1908 is shown here at the Albert Ground in St Kilda Road, Melbourne, headquarters of the Lawn Tennis Association of Victoria at the time. The elegant Edwardian dress of the spectators indicates the social status and importance of the occasion.

Davis Cup Match, Melbourne, 1908

A canoeist and three men in a skiff join two racing crews taking a break from training on the banks of the Yarra, a few kilometres up-river from Melbourne. The youths in the two 4-oared shells might be from the University of Melbourne Rowing Club, or from one of Melbourne's prestigious private schools, Melbourne Grammar or Scotch College. Rowing flourished in early Melbourne. Between 1859 and 1866 five major clubs were formed, including the Melbourne Rowing Club, established in 1862. Its headquarters were in Edward's Boatshed on the banks of the Yarra near Prince's Bridge. In 1876, the Victorian Rowing Association was formed, the first of its kind in the world.

Boating on the Yarra, Melbourne, 1880s

These blokes are clearly about serious men's business. Camped out on the Murray bank, they will eat well off the land, fishing for perch and the fabled Murray cod and shooting rabbits with the shotguns they display as prominently as their fishing rods. No doubt bottled beer is safely stowed in the cool shallows of the river nearby. And they'll be yarning around a camp fire at night, lacing their talk with a few good fish stories, no doubt. Non-commercial fishing in Australia has always been a recreational pastime, one with the added bonus of providing the family with a good feed of fish. Scores of angling clubs now exist around the country, most affiliated with their state angling associations.

Fishing Party on the Murray, Victoria, c. 1910

Except for Melbourne and Geelong, the clubs of the Victorian Football League (now the Australian Football League) were originally closely identified with their suburban headquarters. Teams evoked intense tribal loyalties from local people, and fierce rivalries existed between the clubs and their supporters, particularly between those of neighbouring suburbs. Class could also incite rivalry: patrician Melbourne and working-class Collingwood developed a rivalry, bitter at times, that became a lasting tradition. Here, a huge crowd has turned out to cheer, shout and abuse as Fitzroy does battle with neighbouring Collingwood. The crowd is so dense that the young schoolboy, delighted to be photographed, has to sell his pies and lollies from inside the boundary fence.

Collingwood versus Fitzroy, Melbourne, 1921

The gentleman in action here appears to be showing off to his friends, demonstrating that he can ski the slope without the balancing aid of a ski pole, and that he won't need one to brake with, either. For all of them, the skiing appears to be something of an experiment, judging by their clothing. Kiandra, high in the Snowy Mountains, was the birthplace of Australian skiing. In 1861, Scandinavian gold miners introduced what was then called 'shoe skiing' to the small gold-mining settlement. Soon after, ski races were organised, and Australia's first ski club was formed. Snow shoes were also used as a means of getting around when the town became snow-bound in winter. Today, Kiandra is submerged under Lake Eucumbene, a lake in the Snowy Mountains Scheme.

Snow Skiing at Kiandra, New South Wales, c. 1865

'A very pretty exhibition of archery' said the Melbourne *Herald* of a competition meeting at Emerald Hill (now South Melbourne) in 1855. 'Pretty', and genteel too. So genteel that in 1855, the governor of Victoria organised and hosted the colony's first archery competition in the grounds of Government House. Here, at the Toorak Archery Club in 1905, the local Vicar has given his blessing to the sport, The photograph suggests archery attracted shooters from a cross-section of society, as the varied occupations and the ages of the club members indicate. The sport, however, went into decline in Australia between 1880 and 1920, though not, apparently, in Toorak. The deliberate inclusion of the score sheet in the photograph suggests that this is no frivolous competition.

Kooyong Archery Club, Melbourne, 1908

Champion horse Carbine wins the Melbourne Cup in 1890, carrying a record top weight in the race that today 'stops the nation'. The first Melbourne Cup was run in 1861. It was won by Archer. His owner walked him 800 kilometres to Flemington from his stable in Nowra, New South Wales. Archer won again the following year, a win that proved a boon to the race and to Melbourne. His consecutive wins created great interest in New South Wales, an interest that played a large part in the race becoming the premier national racing event it is today. Archer's 1861 prize was 170 pounds, and a gold watch for his owner. Today, first prize is the gold cup and $3.3 million!

The Melbourne Cup, Flemington, 1890

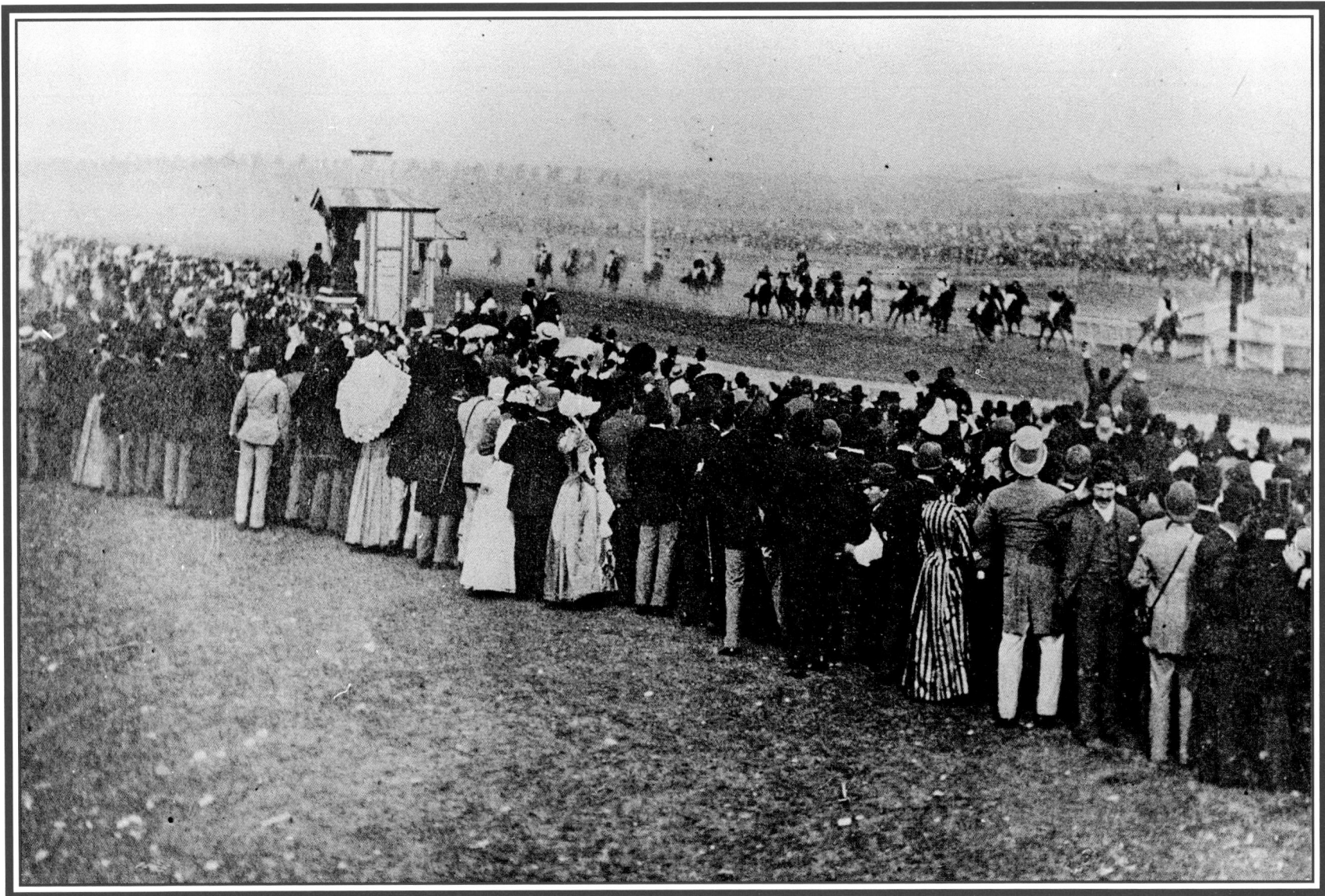

Lifesaving clubs exist primarily to save lives, so lifesavers must spend long hours practising their rescue techniques. The reel, with line and belt, plays a crucial role. Here, watched by an admiring audience, the bronzed Aussies of the day practise their skills. The surfing reel, invented by Lester Ormsby, made its first appearance in December 1906 on Bondi Beach. Sydney's other famous beach, Manly, enjoyed brief notoriety in 1902. Newspaper editor William Goucher advertised that he would defy the law banning daylight bathing by swimming there in public. The law was so unpopular that the police didn't arrest him and the ban was lifted the following year.

Lifesavers Practising at Manly, Sydney, c. 1910

Given that the serious, though limited, reporting of women's cricket in the Australian media is only recent, we could be forgiven for thinking that female involvement in the game is likewise recent. Not so. Women have been playing cricket in Australia since 1874 (and in England since the eighteenth century). Organised state competitions were established throughout Australia in the early 1900s, and a national competition was set up in 1931. Here, the ladies of the Port Elliot Club in South Australia pose proudly for their team photograph, though their elegant Edwardian dresses and broad-brimmed hats would have slowed the pace of their game somewhat. Perhaps the more daring played in bloomers.

Women's Cricket Team, Port Elliot, South Australia, 1908

FAMILY LIFE

Marriage in early Australia was a far more stable institution than it is today. Men and women formed enduring partnerships – husbands as breadwinners and wives as managers of home and family. For the less well-off, particularly those on the land, the whole family often had to pitch in to make a go of it on the farm.

This family is typical of the battlers of the Australian outback, and probably took up land under the Lands Act of 1861; and they have struggled ever since. They could be straight out of Steele Rudd's *On Our Selection*. There's Mum, Dad, their four kids, a son-in-law and three grandchildren. The lasso, the stockwhip and the barn tell us they have some stock, including, perhaps, a horse. No doubt they have dressed in their Sunday best for the photographer, though the men's clothing could do with a good wash. Happily, the children appear well cared for.

Outback Family, c. 1880s

Group wedding photographs like this graced the pianos and mantelpieces of countless Australian homes for most of the twentieth century. And no doubt many still do – if they haven't been consigned to the heirloom cupboard, or found a place on a wall in the home of a child or grandchild of the bride and groom. The groom is from Yarraville, the bride from Footscray – two neighbouring inner-western suburbs of Melbourne. The days of the wedding party being photographed in the local park, gardens or beach are a long way off. And there are no mansion grounds for this middle-class couple. The photographer's studio is their setting, given a touch-up of classical grandeur by the background scene painted on the studio prop.

Footscray Wedding, Melbourne, 1934

Robert Campbell called his homestead Duntroon after the family castle in Scotland. Campbell, a wealthy merchant of early Sydney, was granted the land in 1825 in compensation for the loss of his ship, the *Sydney*, while under charter to the governor of New South Wales to ship food from India to the colony. Duntroon became the social centre of the district surrounding Campbell's huge sheep run. Here, on the croquet lawn of their sumptuous garden, the family is playing host to a group of distinguished guests, including the Bishop of Sydney. Duntroon was on the site chosen in 1909 for the building of Australia's National Capital, Canberra. In 1911 the Australian government acquired the property and established the Royal Military College there.

The Campbells of Duntroon, New South Wales, 1873

In the 1920s a woman's place was unequivocally in the home. If she didn't run her own household herself, she needed the knowledge to oversee the work of her housekeeper. Consequently, domestic science for girls was part of every secondary school curriculum. Calling the subject a science was an attempt to give the study an intellectual rigour, but it consisted essentially of giving the girls the skills to prepare nutritious meals, bake, launder and sew. Evening Continuation Schools offered courses in housekeeping, allied subjects and English to the many girls unable to attend what few high schools there were at that time. Many of the graduates went into service in the larger, wealthier households. Today the subject has a stronger academic content and is also known as home economics or food technology.

Domestic Science Class, c. 1924

This family of Australia's oldest, original people should be photographed, by rights, as part of a much larger, extended family – their clan. They are the product of the program to assimilate Aboriginal people into mainstream Australian culture. The adults were probably brought up in a church mission, educated in its school, and now live on an Aboriginal reserve. Whilst there is much they might be grateful to the mission for, they nevertheless bear the marks of dispossession and the loss of their Indigenous culture. We can be thankful that, at the least, they are together.

Aboriginal Family, 1904

These women are used to food rationing. It's 1946, so they have lived through the period of World War II when coupons were needed to purchase essential goods such as food, clothing and petrol. The women may have to suffer the indignity of standing in line to receive their family's ration of meat, but that's no reason for them not to dress well, and even to wear their jewellery. After all, shopping was an outing. Rationing was introduced in Australia in 1942 to manage shortages of essential goods and to ensure their fair distribution. It was also an attempt to curb inflation and encourage savings in the hope that the money saved would be invested in war bonds. Unfortunately, a black market limited the effectiveness of the scheme.

The Meat Queue, 1946

The store supervisor at Brennan Bros, 'Drapers, Clothiers and Bootmen', of Hannan Street, Kalgoorlie, stands ready to give assistance to the female customers entering his store. The ladies have been given the comfort of bentwood chairs as they carefully examine the bolts of cloth presented to them from the shelves behind the counter. Choosing material for a new dress, curtains, or other household drapery was a matter of no small importance. The women are suitably dressed for the occasion; a visit to town was an important outing in the life of the housewife of that era. Being 1915, perhaps bridal dress material is being chosen for a wedding arranged before the intended groom embarks on a troop ship for the Middle East.

Brennan Bros. Store, Kalgoorlie, Western Australia, c.1915

Walter Burley and Marion Mahoney Griffin were partners in more ways than one. Not only were they husband and wife, they collaborated in a way that has left an indelible mark on Australia's town planning and architectural history. Marion was a brilliant artist and draughtswoman; Walter was an architect and town planner steeped in the current philosophy of the garden city. Both were trained in the office of the great American architect Frank Lloyd Wright. Walter designed the city of Canberra; Marion drew the plans and drawings that played a crucial role in his winning the competition staged to select a design for the new city. They stayed on in Australia, designing houses, housing estates, institutional buildings and the New South Wales towns of Leeton and Griffith.

Walter Burley and Marion Mahoney Griffin, c. 1930

The Pinzone family were amongst the first wave of Italian migrants to enter Australia as refugees escaping poverty and political uncertainty in Italy after World War I. The family established successful businesses in the Victorian towns of Stawell and Ararat. And when they married, they certainly celebrated with true Italian theatricality – the girls' headwear could have come from stage costuming, and there's been no stinting on the flowers. The cast is large, and the players are of the era; the girls are dressed in the flapper style of the 1920s. The Australian government limited Italian migration in the 1920s to prevent a feared dilution of Anglo-Australian culture. It would be another thirty years before we could enjoy fully what the Italians had to offer.

Pinzone Wedding, Victoria, 1927

Sir Donald Bradman, the world's best-ever batsman, was involved in many great batting partnerships on the cricket field. But for him, his greatest partnership was with his wife Jessie (nee Menzies). The two met as youngsters when Jessie stayed at the home of the Bradmans while she attended the Bowral school in New South Wales. Don attended the same school. They met again as young adults in Sydney, fell in love and married on 30 April 1932. From their first home in McMahons Point, Sydney, they moved to Adelaide in 1934, living in the same house for the rest of their lives. The strong bond that united them was broken only when Lady Jessie died in 1997. Sir Donald died in 2001.

Don and Jessie Bradman, 1932

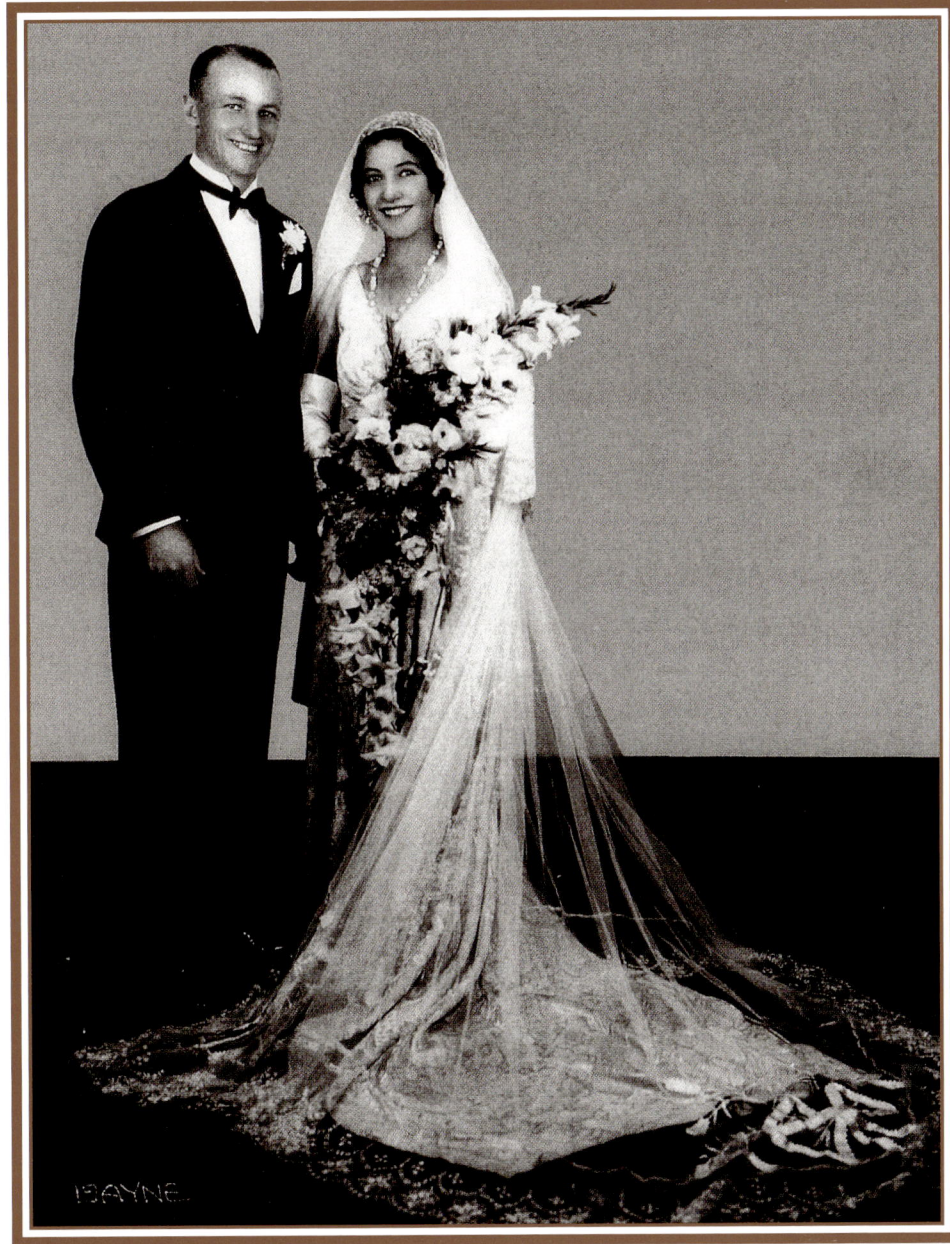

World War I ripped into the heart of countless Australian families. Sixty thousand sons, sweethearts, fathers, brothers and uncles were killed. Many more were injured or maimed for life. It's small wonder that mothers, fathers and sweethearts waited anxiously for the return of those who had survived the carnage. Captured here is the range of emotions of those awaiting a disembarkation. The young woman centre-front looks with hope and expectancy; the older lady squints, searching for the face of a son; the man behind her is on the point of giving way to a smile. One mother is distressed, perhaps because she hasn't yet found the son she looks for in the sea of faces crowded at the rail of the troopship.

Welcoming the Anzacs Home, 1919

Photographed here under the rear pergola of the Lodge, the official Prime Minister's residence in Canberra, are Stanley Bruce and his devoted and supportive wife, Ethel. Stanley Bruce was Australia's eighth and second-youngest Prime Minister, and the first to occupy the Lodge in the new national capital. The couple, of patrician Melbourne background, were well attuned to the elegance and confidence of the 'roaring twenties'. Stanley Bruce, however, lacked empathy with working people, and his government was brought down in 1929 by its mishandling of industrial relations reform. He went on to a long and distinguished career as Australia's high commissioner in London and, in 1947, was granted a peerage to become Lord Bruce of Melbourne. Ethel died in 1967. Bruce, disconsolate, died soon after.

Prime Minister Stanley Bruce and his Wife, Ethel, Canberra, 1928

Artist Norman Lindsay with Rose, his wife, model and muse,
photographed in 1931 at their home in Springwood, New South Wales,
a magnet for writers and artists of the time.